Business Success with Ethics and CSR

Kanchan Thakur

TANEESHA
PUBLISHERS

Title   : Business Success with Ethics and CSR

Author   : Kanchan Thakur

Edition   : 1st (February, 2024)

ISBN   : 9788196942557

Published by

Regd. Add.: 254, Khuriyakhatta No. 10, Bindukhatta,
Lalkuan, Nainital - 262402, Uttarakhand, India
Website : www.taneeshapublishers.in
E-mail : taneeshapublishers@gmail.com
Phone : +91 845481 2712, +91 976041 7980

Printed by :
Manipal Technologies Limited, Bengaluru - 560001, Karnataka

INDEX

Preface

In a time of increased social expectations, ecological demands, and global interconnection, businesses have a more important role than ever in forming a morally and responsibly-minded future. This book explores the various facets of Corporate Social Responsibility (CSR) and places it in the larger, international context of modern business practices.

Businesses now operate on a global scale where social and environmental responsibility are essential to economic success as the world grows more interconnected. This book's chapters weave their way through the complexities of corporate social responsibility, exploring the ways in which companies can work across national boundaries to benefit both the environment and society.

We set out on a journey to investigate the fundamental ideas of corporate social responsibility (CSR) in a globalised environment, with a focus on following international norms and regulations. The story develops to include the critical component of supply chain accountability, acknowledging the worldwide influence of sourcing policies and the interdependence of economies.

Not only do diversity and inclusion become organisational policies, but they also become global imperatives. We explore the difficulty of developing a corporate culture that, while negotiating the complexity of cultural variations and pursuing equity across borders, respects and values diversity on a worldwide basis.

Concerns about environmental sustainability become more important than ever, with an emphasis on CSR projects that tackle issues of global importance like biodiversity preservation and climate change mitigation. The book emphasises how important it is for companies to actively engage in international efforts to stop environmental degradation and to create global environmental goals.

Global operations provide an opportunity to examine human rights, a fundamental component of moral business practices. The conversation goes beyond regional borders, highlighting companies' duties to identify and resolve human rights hazards in many locations.

Dissected as essential elements of CSR initiatives in a globalised environment include partnerships for global development, workforce well-being, and community participation. The story highlights how companies may have a profound impact on the globe when they actively participate in local communities, give their employees a high priority, and create cross-border alliances for sustainable development.

Advocacy and transparent worldwide reporting become indispensable CSR instruments. This book examines the significance of companies being transparent in their reporting procedures and gives stakeholders a thorough understanding of their worldwide influence. It also emphasises how important it is for companies to start acting as change agents by taking part in international discussions and campaigns aimed at building a more just and sustainable world.

We are going to take a journey that questions established ideas and promotes a change to a more accountable and thoughtful way to doing business as we move through these pages. This book offers insights, viewpoints, and practical tactics to help businesses thrive ethically in an interconnected and interdependent global economy. It acts as a guide for companies navigating the complicated landscape of corporate social responsibility in a globalised society.

Chapter 1

Overview of CSR: Philanthropy

Corporate Social Responsibility (CSR) in the context of philanthropy refers to firms making contributions to societal well-being that go beyond their primary economic activities. It extends beyond the pursuit of financial gain to encompass social and environmental considerations. Philanthropic corporate social responsibility (CSR) efforts typically encompass acts of benevolence such as charitable contributions, community development endeavours, and advocacy for social concerns. Companies that participate in philanthropy want to provide a favourable influence on society, improve their public perception, and exhibit a dedication to ethical business principles. Philanthropic corporate social responsibility (CSR) is harmonising profit-driven objectives with a commitment to societal well-being, thereby aligning firms with wider social values.

Corporate Social Responsibility (CSR) has emerged as a crucial element of contemporary business, highlighting a company's dedication to the welfare of society that goes beyond simply making profits. Philanthropy plays a crucial role in the field of Corporate Social Responsibility (CSR), as it represents the active engagement of corporations in making meaningful contributions to society. This comprehensive involvement beyond the conventional economic roles of firms, going beyond the pursuit of profit to tackle social and environmental issues.

Philanthropic corporate social responsibility (CSR) initiatives involve a wide range of activities carried out by firms to promote positive effects on society. Leading these efforts are philanthropic contributions, which entail the distribution of monetary funds to aid different initiatives. Companies leverage their financial resources to make significant contributions to society, whether in the areas of healthcare, education, or disaster assistance. These acts of philanthropy aim to meet urgent needs and contribute to the long-term development of society.

Community development programmes are an additional aspect of charitable corporate social responsibility (CSR). Companies acknowledge the interdependence between their operations and the communities in which they operate. Allocating resources towards local infrastructure, education, and healthcare programmes not only improves the well-being of communities but also fosters a favourable setting for sustainable business practices. Through active engagement in community development, businesses establish a mutually beneficial relationship with the places they serve, promoting shared progress and prosperity.

Furthermore, philanthropic corporate social responsibility (CSR) expands its influence to provide assistance to diverse social concerns. Companies frequently associate themselves with movements and projects that seek to tackle societal issues such as poverty, inequality, and environmental sustainability. Through harnessing their power and assets, businesses assume the role of catalysts for beneficial transformation, actively contributing to the promotion of social equity and the preservation of the environment.

The rationale behind charitable corporate social responsibility (CSR) activities extends beyond pure benevolence. Companies acknowledge the strategic advantages of participating in charity, while also aiming to create a beneficial influence. Improving public perception and brand reputation is a notable motivation. Consumers are progressively favouring businesses that exhibit a dedication to ethical standards and social responsibility. Philanthropy offers a concrete opportunity for firms to demonstrate their commitment to creating a significant impact in the world.

Moreover, philanthropic corporate social responsibility (CSR) efforts have a significant role in fostering trust among stakeholders, including as consumers, employees, and investors. A corporation that actively engages in philanthropy demonstrates a responsible approach to conducting business, by matching its values with those of its stakeholders. This alignment cultivates employee loyalty and pride, appeals to socially conscious consumers, and potentially impacts investment choices in a good manner.

The notion of "shared value," as initially proposed by Michael Porter and Mark Kramer, encompasses the premise that firms have the capacity to generate economic benefit for shareholders while also serving the needs of society. Philanthropic corporate social responsibility (CSR) embraces this concept by incorporating both social and economic factors. Companies acknowledge that sustainable business operations must encompass more than only generating profits, but also entail a wider obligation towards the welfare of society.

Achieving a harmonious integration of philanthropic efforts with essential business operations necessitates a deliberate and strategic approach. Companies must intentionally choose causes and activities that are in line with their beliefs, industry, and the concerns of their stakeholders. This strategic connection guarantees that philanthropic endeavours resonate really and contribute to significant, enduring transformation.

It is crucial to acknowledge that philanthropic corporate social responsibility (CSR) is but one aspect of a comprehensive CSR strategy.

The wider scope of corporate social responsibility (CSR) include environmental sustainability, ethical conduct in business operations, and active involvement with stakeholders. Companies dedicated to comprehensive corporate social responsibility (CSR) acknowledge that philanthropy in isolation is insufficient to tackle the intricate societal concerns. Furthermore, it enhances and strengthens existing CSR activities, so establishing a more comprehensive structure for ethical business practices.

CSR: Conventional and strategic approach

Within the domain of Corporate Social Responsibility (CSR), the conventional and strategic viewpoints represent two separate paradigms that outline different approaches to how firms interact with societal well-being.

The traditional approach to corporate social responsibility (CSR) sometimes entails irregular and impromptu philanthropic endeavours. Companies, motivated by a sense of philanthropic responsibility, may provide grants or support community activities without a well-defined strategy. Although these programmes have good intentions, they usually adopt a reactive approach by addressing current needs or crisis situations. The emphasis is placed on charity rather than integrating philanthropy with wider corporate goals. The traditional method employed here fails to incorporate CSR into the fundamental business plan in a systematic manner, potentially limiting the ability to fully capitalise on the good effects on both society and the enterprise.

On the other hand, the strategic approach to CSR considers philanthropy as a purposeful and essential component of the broader company plan. Companies that embrace this approach ensure that their charitable endeavours are in line with their fundamental principles, industry environment, and the interests of their stakeholders. Strategic philanthropy entails a deliberate choice of causes and programmes that not only help to the overall welfare of society but also align genuinely with the company's mission. The focus is on establishing shared value, where societal and economic goals are aligned to attain sustainable results.

Strategic giving extends beyond isolated contributions or local initiatives. It requires a sustained dedication to tackling systemic problems and generating beneficial transformation. This approach acknowledges the interdependence between a company's prosperity and the welfare of the community it caters to. For example, a technology corporation that specialises in education may strategically allocate funds towards initiatives that advance digital literacy, thereby connecting its philanthropic endeavours with its business acumen.

Furthermore, strategic philanthropy incorporates corporate social responsibility (CSR) into the decision-making procedures of a company. Companies evaluate the social and environmental consequences of their activities and strive to utilise their main strengths for the betterment of society. By adopting a proactive approach, firms can actively contribute to sustainable growth while effectively managing possible risks related to social and environmental concerns.

From a traditional perspective, Corporate Social Responsibility (CSR) is perceived as a distinct and frequently secondary activity, lacking integration with the primary company functions. Philanthropy can be seen as a moral duty rather than a strategic necessity. On the other hand, the strategic viewpoint acknowledges that appropriate corporate activities, such as charity, are essential for achieving long-term success. Companies that adopt strategic philanthropy recognise that it involves more than just charitable giving; it also entails generating value for both society and the business.

The conventional and strategic viewpoints on Corporate Social Responsibility (CSR), specifically in relation to philanthropy, embody two distinct and contrasting approaches. The conventional approach to philanthropy consists of occasional and reactive charity efforts. In contrast, the strategic method entails integrating philanthropy into the core corporate strategy, aligning it with values, objectives, and stakeholder expectations. The transition from traditional to strategic philanthropy represents a wider transformation in how firms understand and address their social obligations, acknowledging the intrinsic connection between corporate prosperity and society well.

Environmental concerns within the context of business ethics and corporate social responsibility

In today's corporate world, the convergence of business ethics and Corporate Social Responsibility (CSR) is primarily characterised by a strong dedication to environmental sustainability. As firms confront the ethical ramifications of their activities, environmental considerations have become a crucial aspect of corporate social responsibility (CSR). This essay delves into the complex environmental issues associated with business ethics and corporate social responsibility (CSR), analysing the difficulties, ethical factors, and the changing role of firms in tackling these urgent concerns.

Environmental Degradation and Ethical Implications: An important environmental challenge that businesses face is the widespread issue of environmental degradation. Activities such as deforestation, pollution, and resource depletion are responsible for the degradation of ecosystems and natural habitats. Businesses that engage in environmentally harmful practices are subject to ethical scrutiny due to their influence on biodiversity, climate change, and ecological equilibrium. This raises a basic ethical inquiry: to what degree are firms accountable for the environmental repercussions of their activities?

Management of waste and mitigation of pollution: Waste management and pollution are significant concerns that have serious ethical ramifications. The improper disposal of industrial waste, the release of pollutants, and the use of non-biodegradable materials are all factors that contribute to the contamination of soil, air, and water. Businesses must confront the ethical obligation of reducing their impact on the environment, guaranteeing that their activities do not harm ecosystems or endanger human health. Companies that follow ethical business practices actively pursue sustainable waste management solutions and implement cleaner production methods to minimise their environmental footprint.

Climate change: The phenomenon of climate change is closely linked to the release of greenhouse gases into the atmosphere. The ethical aspect of climate change has emerged as a central topic in discussions pertaining to business ethics and corporate social responsibility (CSR). Industrial operations emit greenhouse gases that have a substantial impact on climate change, resulting in negative consequences such as increased temperatures, severe weather events, and the rise of sea levels. Companies are facing growing responsibility for their carbon emissions, which raises ethical concerns over their impact on global environmental issues. Ethical enterprises see the pressing need to address climate change and frequently establish aggressive goals to decrease emissions and shift towards sustainable energy sources.

Depletion of resources and the implementation of sustainable practices: Businesses must prioritise the ethical utilisation of natural resources as a crucial component of their environmental responsibilities.

The ethical implications of practices that result in resource depletion, such as excessive extraction of water or irresponsible harvesting of forests, are raised due to their detrimental effects on ecosystems and potential consequences for future generations. Ethical enterprises demonstrate a steadfast dedication to embracing sustainable methodologies, such as conscientious procurement of resources, incorporation of circular economy ideas, and prioritisation of resource preservation. These methods are in line with the ethical need to guarantee the long-term sustainability and durability of ecosystems, as well as the fair allocation of resources.

Preservation of Biodiversity: Biodiversity loss is a critical environmental problem that carries substantial ethical consequences. enterprises engaging in business operations that intrude upon natural ecosystems or contribute to the decline of biodiversity prompt inquiries regarding the ethical obligation of these enterprises. Ethical considerations encompass safeguarding endangered species, conserving ecosystems, and recognising the interdependence between biodiversity and human welfare. Companies that prioritise corporate social responsibility (CSR) frequently participate in biodiversity conservation endeavours, providing support for initiatives that promote the preservation and rehabilitation of natural ecosystems.

Commitment to regulation and ethical principles: The ethical aspects of environmental challenges are intricately linked to the observance of legal requirements and the commitment to ethical principles. Companies have ethical quandaries when manoeuvring within regulatory systems, particularly in regions where environmental rules may be lenient. Ethical enterprises acknowledge that adhering to environmental regulations is a fundamental requirement, but they surpass legal obligations by setting elevated ethical benchmarks for environmental care. This proactive strategy entails integrating environmental ethics into the company culture, policy, and decision-making processes.

Engaging stakeholders and promoting transparency: Businesses must consider ethical implications while tackling environmental challenges, including how they interact with stakeholders and convey their environmental practices. Providing clear and comprehensive information about environmental performance, including sharing details of environmental impact assessments, showcases a dedication to ethical business conduct. Interacting with stakeholders, such as local communities, environmental organisations, and investors, promotes responsibility and guarantees that a wide range of viewpoints are taken into account when developing environmental plans. Ethical enterprises acknowledge the significance of engaging with stakeholders to improve environmental accountability and resolve the issues made by diverse stakeholders.

The Changing Role of Businesses in Environmental Accountability: The changing role of businesses in tackling environmental challenges signifies a wider transition towards a more sustainable and ethical approach to corporate behaviour. As public demands for environmental responsibility increase, firms are obligated to include sustainability into their fundamental business plans. Ethical enterprises acknowledge the inherent connection between environmental sustainability and sustained corporate prosperity. Embracing environmentally friendly technologies, applying circular economy ideas, and striving towards carbon neutrality are clear indications of a proactive stance towards environmental responsibility.

The environmental concerns associated with corporate ethics and Corporate Social Responsibility involve a range of difficulties that organisations must traverse in the intricate global context of today. Companies' operations are significantly influenced by ethical considerations, which encompass managing pollution, waste management, reducing climate change, and conserving biodiversity. In light of global environmental issues, there is a growing need for corporations to surpass mere regulatory compliance and adopt a proactive and ethical approach to sustainability. The convergence of business ethics, corporate social responsibility (CSR), and environmental stewardship not only signifies a dedication to moral behaviour but also establishes corporations as catalysts for constructive transformation, so fostering a more enduring and adaptable future for both commerce and the environment.

Societal concerns within the realm of business ethics and corporate social responsibility

The convergence of corporate ethics and Corporate societal Responsibility (CSR) is a dynamic and evolving domain that spans a wide range of societal concerns. Given the significant influence of companies on society, ethical concerns of social responsibility have become increasingly important. This essay delves into prominent societal concerns in the fields of business ethics and corporate social responsibility (CSR), analysing obstacles, ethical deliberations, and the changing role of corporations in tackling these urgent issues.

Labour Practices and Ethical Employment: A fundamental concern in the field of business ethics is how workers are treated and the commitment to ethical employment practices. Businesses have a moral obligation to guarantee equitable compensation, secure working environments, and uphold labour rights. Unethical labour practices, including the exploitation of workers, discrimination, and the provision of unsafe working conditions, not only infringe upon human rights but also damage a company's reputation. Ethical enterprises prioritise the welfare of its employees, acknowledging that a robust and engaged staff is essential for long-term prosperity.

Diversity and Inclusion: Diversity and inclusion have become as prominent social concerns in recent years. Ethical enterprises recognise the significance of establishing work environments that embody diversity, fairness, and inclusivity. Engaging in discrimination, whether it be on the basis of colour, gender, ethnicity, or other criteria, not only violates ethical values but also carries the risk of legal repercussions and harm to a company's reputation. Ethical issues encompass the establishment of policies that promote diversity, guaranteeing equitable opportunities, and cultivating an inclusive corporate culture that embraces and values differences.

Human Rights and Supply Chain Ethics: The globalisation of supply networks poses ethical dilemmas concerning human rights. Businesses must strategically traverse intricate supply networks to ensure that their products are not linked to unethical labour practices, coerced labour, or violations of human rights. Ethical considerations in supply chain management encompass the principles of transparency, responsibility, and a dedication to ensuring that suppliers comply with ethical norms. Companies that prioritise corporate social responsibility (CSR) conduct thorough investigations to identify and address any violations of human rights occurring in their supply chains.

Community Engagement and Impact: Businesses play a crucial role in communities, and their activities can have a substantial influence on local citizens. Ethical considerations encompass the principles of transparency and respect when interacting with communities, as well as the efforts to minimise adverse effects like pollution or displacement, and the active contribution to community development. CSR efforts focused on strengthening local communities, promoting education, and tackling social concerns exemplify a dedication to ethical company practices that go beyond mere profit generation.

Consumer Protection and Product Safety: Responsible businesses give priority to safeguarding consumers and ensuring the safety of their products. Ensuring the safety and quality of products is both a legal obligation and an ethical duty. Transparency in labelling, ensuring the provision of precise information, and immediately resolving concerns regarding product safety are crucial ethical factors. Businesses that place consumer well-being as a top priority establish trust with their client base, establishing enduring relationships founded on honesty and dependability.

Ethical Marketing Practices: Marketing is a potent instrument employed by firms to engage in communication with consumers. Nevertheless, ethical issues play a crucial role in marketing strategies. Untruthful advertising, dishonest marketing strategies, or manipulation of consumer perceptions are in violation of ethical precepts. Ethical marketing encompasses the principles of open and honest communication, accurate portrayal of products, and upholding the independence of customers to make well-informed decisions.

Philanthropy and societal Impact: Although philanthropy is commonly linked to beneficial societal outcomes, ethical concerns emerge around how firms engage in charity endeavours. Ethical philanthropy entails directing donations and activities towards actual community needs, rather than seeking superficial public relations advantages. Ethical philanthropy is fostered by transparent reporting of charitable efforts, ensuring the monies are directed to the intended beneficiaries, and actively seeking input from communities.

Access to Healthcare and Affordable Products: Ensuring access to critical products and services is an ethical concern for firms operating in industries such as pharmaceuticals and healthcare. Ethical enterprises acknowledge the significance of offering cost-effective healthcare solutions and indispensable goods, hence contributing to enhanced public health results. The availability of drugs, vaccines, and healthcare services is crucial in resolving social disparities.

Education and Skill Development: Education and skill development are important areas that ethical firms prioritise in order to contribute to the overall growth of society. This include providing assistance to educational initiatives, grants, and vocational instruction that empower individuals and communities. The ethical obligation is not alone to provide the workforce with essential abilities, but also to tackle wider societal issues pertaining to educational disparity and accessibility.

Technology and Ethical Innovation: Technology and ethical innovation provide significant challenges for firms in the digital world. Matters such as the protection of data privacy, the presence of algorithmic biases, and the consequences of automation on employment necessitate meticulous ethical examination. Technology companies dedicated to corporate social responsibility (CSR) see their obligation to ethically drive innovation, placing societal welfare as a priority and refraining from causing harm to persons or communities.

Obstacles and Ethical Dilemmas: Businesses strive to ethically tackle societal concerns, yet they frequently encounter obstacles and ethical quandaries. The act of reconciling profit-driven objectives with ethical considerations, particularly in fiercely competitive marketplaces, can give rise to conflicts and strains. Companies may encounter ethical issues when they are faced with decisions that have varying impacts on stakeholders, necessitating thoughtful evaluation of conflicting interests.

Decisions about layoffs, pricing schemes, or supplier relationships might provide ethical dilemmas.

Furthermore, companies that operate in multiple international environments must effectively navigate through different cultural norms, legal frameworks, and societal expectations. What is seen ethically acceptable in one geographical area may be perceived differently in another. Ethical enterprises acknowledge the significance of cultural sensitivity and adapt their strategies to conform with the principles of the local communities in which they conduct their operations.

The Changing Role of Businesses in Social Responsibility

The changing involvement of corporations in tackling social concerns is indicative of a wider trend towards a comprehensive and socially accountable strategy. Ethical enterprises acknowledge the interdependence between societal welfare and corporate prosperity. Corporate executives are increasingly considering Corporate Social Responsibility (CSR) as an essential component of their business strategy, rather than a distinct charity effort. The subsequent patterns exemplify the expanding function of businesses in social responsibility:

Integration into company Strategy: Ethical considerations are no longer confined to distinct Corporate Social Responsibility (CSR) programmes, but rather they are included into the fundamental company strategy. Businesses acknowledge that ethical practices are conducive to sustained success, as they cultivate consumer loyalty, recruit high-caliber staff, and mitigate risks linked with social concerns. By incorporating ethical considerations into strategic decision-making, corporations can proactively tackle societal challenges instead of only reacting to crises.

Stakeholder Engagement: Stakeholder engagement is becoming increasingly important for businesses as a way to comprehend and tackle social challenges. By actively involving a wide array of stakeholders, such as employees, consumers, communities, and advocacy groups, transparency is promoted and multiple viewpoints are taken into account. Ethical enterprises proactively solicit input from stakeholders and integrate their views into decision-making procedures.

Transparency and Reporting: Transparency and reporting are essential components of ethical business conduct. Corporations are progressively more open and forthcoming regarding their societal influence, moral principles, and endeavours to tackle social problems. Thorough coverage of corporate social responsibility (CSR) endeavours, environmental achievements, and societal influence offers stakeholders a precise comprehension of a company's dedication to ethical behaviour. Transparent communication is a key priority for ethical firms as it helps to establish trust with stakeholders.

Ethical Leadership: Leadership is essential in influencing the ethical culture of an organisation. Ethical leaders place a high importance on fulfilling their social obligations, establishing the overall atmosphere inside the organisation, and exerting their influence on decision-making at all levels. Ethical leadership entails a steadfast dedication to principles, honesty, and a sincere aspiration to make a constructive impact on society. Companies led by ethical individuals are more inclined to handle social concerns in a responsible and proactive manner.

Collaboration and Partnerships: Collaboration and partnerships are necessary when tackling intricate socioeconomic problems. Ethical enterprises acknowledge the impossibility of addressing societal issues in solitude and aggressively pursue partnerships with non-profit organisations, governmental agencies, and other corporations. Cooperative endeavours enhance the influence of social responsibility projects, resulting in more extensive and enduring results.

The domains of business ethics and Corporate Social Responsibility (CSR) encompass a complex terrain that necessitates firms to confront obstacles, make ethical choices, and adapt their responsibilities as conscientious contributors to society welfare. This section has examined a wide range of social issues, including labour practices, diversity and inclusion, human rights in the supply chain, community engagement, consumer protection, ethical marketing, philanthropy, healthcare accessibility, education, and the ethical implications of technological innovation.

The moral obligation for corporations to tackle these social challenges is evident - it extends beyond mere adherence to the law and corresponds with wider community anticipations. Ethical enterprises acknowledge that their activities have extensive effects on several stakeholders, and therefore use a proactive approach to social responsibility. Businesses exhibit a dedication to ethical behaviour by giving importance to equitable labour practices, advocating for diversity and inclusion, guaranteeing ethical practices throughout their supplier chain, actively participating in community engagement, and making contributions to societal development.

The complexities of addressing social issues in varied worldwide contexts are highlighted by the challenges and ethical concerns faced by corporations. Achieving a harmonious equilibrium between financial incentives and moral considerations, particularly in highly competitive marketplaces, necessitates deliberate and judicious decision-making. The ever-changing public expectations, cultural subtleties, and shifting conventions emphasise the importance for businesses to stay alert and flexible in their approach to social responsibility.

The changing role of businesses in social responsibility is indicative of a larger pattern where companies perceive CSR as a fundamental component of their overall strategy rather than a secondary undertaking. The contemporary environment of socially responsible organisations is characterised by the incorporation of ethical issues into company strategy, stakeholder involvement, transparent reporting, ethical leadership, and collaborative collaborations.

In the future, corporations are expected to further develop their approach to solving societal challenges. Recent developments indicate that ethical issues will have a progressively significant impact on moulding corporate behaviour. The convergence of business ethics, corporate social responsibility (CSR), and social responsibility not only positions firms as accountable contributors to the overall welfare of society but also offers a structured framework for enduring, morally upright business operations.

As corporations traverse the complex landscape of social issues, the decisions they make have far-reaching effects beyond their financial gains. Ethical enterprises actively contribute to promoting positive societal transformation, cultivate trust among stakeholders, and establish robust and sustainable operational practices. The correlation between ethical behaviour and corporate prosperity highlights the significant impact that firms may have when they adopt their responsibility as ethical guardians within the wider framework of society. The pursuit of social responsibility is a perpetual and ever-changing process that necessitates a steadfast dedication to ethical values, as firms endeavour to make a beneficial influence on their surroundings.

Labour issues in the realm of ethical business practices and corporate social responsibility

Within the domain of corporate ethics and Corporate Social

Responsibility (CSR), labour issues are a crucial and intricate aspect. Businesses must prioritise the treatment of workers, the strict adherence to ethical employment practices, and the wider societal ramifications of labour practices. This essay examines labor-related difficulties, ethical considerations, and the changing role of businesses in dealing with workforce management challenges.

Fair Wages and Living Wage: Equitable compensation and the provision of a living wage are essential ethical obligations for enterprises. The notion of fair wages goes beyond mere adherence to the law and encompasses compensation that ensures employees a satisfactory level of living. Companies dedicated to corporate social responsibility (CSR) acknowledge the significance of providing equitable salaries that allow workers to fulfil their essential requirements, sustain their families, and actively engage in their localities. The ethical aspect entails tackling income inequality and advocating for fair compensation systems that accurately reflect the worth of employees' contributions.

Safe Working Conditions: Ensuring safe working conditions is a fundamental aspect of ethical employment practices. Businesses have a moral duty to guarantee that employees are not subjected to avoidable dangers or perils that could jeopardise their physical and mental welfare. Ethical issues encompass conducting routine evaluations of workplace safety, providing comprehensive instruction on safety procedures, and executing preventive steps to avert accidents or occupational ailments. A moral stance towards ensuring secure working conditions demonstrates a dedication to the respect and well-being of workers.

Labor Rights and Unionization: Ensuring labour rights and the freedom to unionise is a fundamental ethical concern for firms. Employees possess the entitlement to engage in organising, engaging in collective bargaining, and advocating for their interests without experiencing any form of retaliation. Ethical enterprises cultivate a conducive atmosphere that upholds the entitlements of employees to establish labour unions and participate in collective bargaining to secure equitable remuneration, working circumstances, and other aspects of employment. The ethical treatment of employees entails acknowledging and adhering to the norms established in global labour standards.

Elimination of Forced Labor: The eradication of forced labour is an ethical obligation that cannot be compromised. Businesses must ensure that their operations and supply networks are devoid of any manifestation of coerced or involuntary labour. Ethical issues encompass the diligent examination and resolution of cases of coerced labour within the organisation or its extended supplier chain. Companies dedicated to corporate social responsibility (CSR) actively strive to eliminate the practice of modern slavery and maintain the dignity and rights of their employees.

Non-Discrimination and Equal Opportunities: Ensuring non-discrimination and fair chances for all employees is a fundamental ethical obligation. Businesses ought to establish inclusive work environments that are devoid of any form of discrimination, be it related to race, gender, age, religion, sexual orientation, or any other distinguishing trait. Ethical employment practices encompass the implementation of rules that promote diversity and inclusion, guaranteeing equitable access to opportunities, and eliminating biases that could impede career progression. Companies dedicated to corporate social responsibility (CSR) acknowledge the inherent worth of having a workforce that is diverse and inclusive.

Work-Life Balance: Maintaining a harmonious equilibrium between professional responsibilities and personal life is an ethical concern that has a direct influence on the welfare of employees. Ethical enterprises acknowledge the significance of cultivating a robust equilibrium between work and personal life to mitigate the risks of exhaustion, anxiety, and psychological well-being challenges. Enforcing adaptable work schedules, fostering a culture that values individuals' personal time, and offering assistance for employee welfare all contribute to an ethical approach to managing the workforce.

Child Labour Prevention: The moral proscription of child labour is a basic labour concern that firms must confront. It is morally necessary to ensure that no kid is subjected to exploitative labour practices. Responsible businesses adopt rigorous procedures to authenticate the age of their workers, particularly in sectors where the exploitation of child labour is widespread. Moreover, ethical considerations encompass supply chain management, necessitating organisations to implement measures to proactively avoid and eradicate child labour across their whole value chain.

Employee Benefits and Social Protection: Employee benefits and social protection are essential obligations for businesses, as they have a moral duty to provide complete support in these areas. Ethical employment practices encompass more than just compensation considerations, extending to encompass perks such as health insurance, retirement programmes, and other types of social security. Companies dedicated to corporate social responsibility (CSR) understand that promoting the welfare of their employees includes providing access to vital services and safeguarding against economic risks.

Ethical considerations in the management of the workforce: Ethically addressing labour concerns necessitates a holistic approach to managing the workforce. Relevant ethical factors in this particular situation encompass:

Employment Policy Transparency: Ethical enterprises prioritise transparency in their employment rules, guaranteeing that employees possess a clear comprehension of their entitlements, advantages, and obligations. Open and clear communication promotes trust and guarantees that employees are well-informed about the terms and conditions of their employment.

Employee Engagement and Feedback: Employee engagement and feedback are integral to ethical workforce management, as it entails actively involving employees and soliciting their input. Businesses ought to establish channels for employees to express their concerns, offer feedback on decision-making procedures, and contribute to the enhancement of working conditions.

Investment in Employee Development: Ethical enterprises allocate resources towards enhancing the professional growth and skills of their workforce. This include the provision of training opportunities, career progression programmes, and skill-building activities that contribute to the development and satisfaction of employees in their respective positions.

Whistleblower Protection: Whistleblower protection encompasses ethical considerations. It is imperative for businesses to establish systems that safeguard employees who disclose unethical activities or infractions occurring within the organisation. Whistleblower protection promotes a culture characterised by responsibility and honesty.

Social Dialogue and Collective Bargaining: Businesses dedicated to ethical labour practices regularly participate in societal dialogue and endorse collective bargaining procedures. Ethical issues encompass the acknowledgement of the significance of transparent communication, bargaining, and cooperation between employers and employees in order to tackle mutual concerns.

Community Engagement: Community participation is an integral part of ethical workforce management. Businesses ought to actively participate in the communities where they operate, by providing assistance to local development efforts, education, and social welfare programmes that benefit both employees and the wider community.

Continuous improvement is a fundamental aspect of ethical firms, since they actively foster a culture of enhancing worker management. This entails consistently evaluating and improving policies and practices to conform to changing ethical norms, societal demands, and the welfare of employees.

The Changing Role of Businesses in Tackling Labour Issues:

The role of corporations in resolving labour issues has undergone substantial changes, reflecting shifting public expectations and an increasing recognition of the interdependence between ethical worker management and sustained company prosperity. Key developments demonstrate the changing role of businesses in tackling labor-related challenges:

Human-Centric Approach: The changing role of businesses places a stronger emphasis on a workforce management approach that prioritises the needs and well-being of employees. Businesses are placing greater importance on employee well-being, pleasure, and professional growth as essential components of their entire strategy, acknowledging people as valuable resources.

Technology and Workforce Dynamics: The progress in technology and evolving workforce dynamics are influencing how businesses address labour concerns. The prevalence of remote work, adaptable schedules, and digital communication tools demonstrates an awareness of the developing nature of work and the significance of adjusting to the changing requirements of employees.

Social Impact and Stakeholder Expectations: Companies are increasingly aware of the social consequences of their employment policies. Businesses are being compelled to embrace more ethical and socially responsible workforce management practices due to the influence of stakeholder expectations, which encompass employees, consumers, and investors.

Integration of CSR into Core Business Strategy: The incorporation of Corporate Social Responsibility (CSR) into the fundamental company strategy is a prominent and noteworthy trend. Ethical labour practices are considered essential not only for meeting legal requirements, but also as strategic necessities that enhance a positive corporate culture, foster employee loyalty, and bolster brand reputation.

Globalisation and supplier Chain Responsibility: The process of globalisation has increased the necessity for corporations to assume accountability for labour standards, not only inside their own immediate operations, but also across their whole supplier networks. Businesses are increasingly required to maintain labour standards globally in order to adhere to ethical issues in workforce management, even in foreign situations.

Governmental concerns regarding business ethics and corporate social responsibility

Governmental matters are of utmost importance in defining the ethical environment in which businesses function. They have a significant impact on rules, regulations, and expectations for business behaviour. The convergence of business ethics and Corporate Social Responsibility (CSR) with governmental issues is a dynamic field that involves a wide range of factors. This essay examines important governmental concerns, ethical deliberations, and the changing role of corporations in managing the intricate connection between government legislation and ethical business conduct.

Regulatory Compliance and Ethical Business Conduct: Regulatory compliance and ethical business conduct are essential for businesses to operate within the legal framework established by government rules. Ensuring adherence to regulations is not just a legal obligation but also a fundamental aspect of ethical business behaviour. Ethical issues encompass comprehending, sticking to, and occasionally beyond the basic legal requirements established by governing bodies. Ethical enterprises acknowledge the significance of conscientiously negotiating the regulatory environment with honesty and a dedication to maintaining the essence of the legislation.

Anti-Corruption Measures: Governmental matters concerning anti-corruption measures have significant ramifications for business ethics. Corruption presents a substantial menace to the practice of ethical business, since it undermines confidence, distorts markets, and obstructs economic progress. Authorities enforce anti-corruption legislation and transparency programmes as means to suppress corrupt practices. Ethical enterprises proactively participate in anti-corruption endeavours, establishing strong compliance initiatives, performing thorough investigations, and fostering a climate of openness and honesty.

Taxation and Ethical Business procedures: Taxation policy and procedures are essential matters of government that overlap with the ethical conduct of businesses. Ethical considerations encompass the transparent fulfilment of tax obligations, the avoidance of tax evasion, and the active contribution to the societies in which enterprises operate. The ethical dimension is firms recognising their responsibility in upholding public services by engaging in fair and reasonable tax methods, rather than taking advantage of legal loopholes to avoid taxes.

Environmental Regulations and Sustainability: The implementation of governmental legislation pertaining to environmental protection and sustainability is a crucial factor that significantly impacts ethical business operations. Ethical enterprises acknowledge the significance of adhering to environmental regulations and actively participate in sustainability endeavours. In accordance with governmental objectives to mitigate climate change, decrease carbon emissions, and save natural resources, ethical enterprises frequently establish ambitious environmental objectives that surpass legislative mandates.

Consumer Protection Laws: Consumer protection regulations, which are governed by the government, have a significant impact on the ethical environment in which firms engage with consumers. Ethical issues encompass principles such as open and honest communication, equitable advertising tactics, and the delivery of secure and high-quality products. Ethical corporations not only adhere to consumer protection regulations but also actively tackle consumer issues, prioritise product safety, and engage in equitable and truthful marketing tactics.

Human Rights and Labor Laws: The ethical conduct of businesses is greatly influenced by governmental restrictions concerning human rights and labour legislation. Businesses are required to adhere to regulations that control equitable labour practices, absence of prejudice, and occupational safety. Ethical issues encompass the preservation of workers' rights, the promotion of diversity and inclusion, and the proactive eradication of forced labour both within the organisation and throughout its supply chain.

Data Protection and Privacy Laws: Data protection and privacy laws have gained significant importance in government due to the growing dependence on technology. These laws address ethical concerns associated with safeguarding data and maintaining privacy. Businesses are responsible for protecting sensitive personal information, and ethical considerations include preserving privacy, ensuring data security, and adhering to any rules. Responsible firms give priority to strong data protection measures, clear data policies, and the preservation of individuals' privacy rights.

Access to Education and Skills Development: The impact of governmental concerns concerning education policy and skills development programmes on enterprises is mostly seen in terms of the readiness of the workforce. Ethical concerns encompass the cooperation between corporations and governments to promote educational programmes, enhance skills acquisition, and tackle societal issues pertaining to the availability of high-quality education. Ethical enterprises acknowledge the significance of allocating resources towards the cultivation of a proficient and knowledgeable labour force, with the aim of reaping enduring societal and economic advantages.

Healthcare policies and their impact on the well-being of employees:
The ethical treatment and well-being of employees are influenced by governmental problems pertaining to healthcare legislation. Ethical considerations encompass the provision of healthcare benefits, the promotion of a conducive work environment, and adherence to health and safety requirements. Ethical enterprises see the inherent connection between the welfare of their employees and the overall prosperity of their organisation. They actively participate in healthcare initiatives and advocate for policies that promote public health.

Corporate Governance and Accountability: Corporate governance and accountability pertain to governmental matters concerning regulations that establish the structure and oversight of business management and ensure responsibility. Ethical considerations encompass the makeup of governing boards, the openness of decision-making processes, and the establishment of systems to ensure leaders are held responsible for their conduct. Ethical enterprises implement robust corporate governance measures, which guarantee honesty, responsibility, and congruence with the concerns of diverse stakeholders.

Ethical considerations while dealing with governmental issues: Ensuring ethical practices in dealing with government bodies and conducting operations is crucial for firms to address governmental challenges. Key ethical considerations while dealing with governmental issues encompass:

Participating in Advocacy and Collaboration: Ethical firms proactively involve themselves in advocacy endeavours to influence policies and regulations that are in line with ethical business principles. Engaging in partnerships with government bodies, industry groups, and non-governmental organisations enables firms to actively participate in shaping policies that prioritise ethical behaviour.

Transparency and Reporting: Ethical enterprises place a high value on openness and honesty in their dealings with governmental institutions. This entails furnishing precise information, revealing pertinent data, and complying with reporting obligations. Open and clear communication promotes trust and holds corporations responsible for their actions.

Comprehensive Compliance Programs: Comprehensive compliance programmes are implemented by ethical firms, surpassing the basic legal standards. These programmes encompass routine audits, instructional sessions, and internal checks to guarantee compliance with ethical standards and governmental legislation.

Ethical Decision-Making in Policy Advocacy: When participating in policy advocacy, morally upright firms take into account the wider societal consequences of proposed rules. Ethical decision-making entails evaluating the extent to which policies adhere to ideals of equity, impartiality, and the welfare of various stakeholders.

Responsible Lobbying Practices: Responsible lobbying practices encompass ethical considerations. Businesses involved in government advocacy must ensure that their lobbying activities are transparent, comply with ethical guidelines, and prioritise the public interest over specific company interests.

Advocating for Ethical Leadership: Ethical enterprises acknowledge the significance of endorsing and fostering ethical leadership within their establishments. This entails cultivating a company culture that places importance on honesty, responsibility, and prudent decision-making. Businesses rely on ethical leaders to champion ethical behaviour and facilitate communication between the organisation and government bodies.

Corporate Social Responsibility Programs: Companies dedicated to ethical behaviour frequently incorporate Corporate Social Responsibility (CSR) programmes into their activities. These programmes are in line with the demands of society, tackle environmental and social concerns, and enhance the well-being of communities. Ethical enterprises perceive corporate social responsibility (CSR) not as a basic duty, but as a chance to create a favourable influence that extends beyond legislative mandates.

The Changing Role of Businesses in Addressing Governmental Issues

The role of corporations in addressing governmental concerns is undergoing a transformation, influenced by shifting public expectations, heightened knowledge of ethical considerations, and the acknowledgment of the interconnectedness between commercial success and ethical behaviour. Key developments demonstrate the changing role of corporations in dealing with governmental matters:

Stakeholder engagement and collaboration: engagement and collaboration have become increasingly important for businesses, as they prioritise working closely with government entities. Businesses actively solicit feedback from a variety of stakeholders, including as consumers, employees, non-governmental organisations, and the wider society, because they recognise that varied perspectives enhance decision-making.

Global Collaboration on Ethical Standards: In the context of businesses operating in a more interconnected global environment, there is a rising inclination towards worldwide cooperation over ethical standards. The existence of industry-specific ethical frameworks, international agreements, and activities that go beyond national borders demonstrates the understanding that ethical considerations necessitate a cooperative and unified approach.

Technology and Ethical Governance: Technological advancements offer potential benefits and difficulties for firms in managing governmental matters. The adoption of technology to facilitate transparent reporting, safeguard data, and ensure ethical governance is a prevailing trend that corresponds to the changing landscape of ethical business practices.

Focus on Environmental and Social Impact: Businesses are progressively acknowledging the significance of taking into account their environmental and social impact when developing governmental regulations. Ethical considerations cover not only current corporate operations but also broader contributions to sustainability, social development, and responsible resource management.

Advocacy for Ethical Governance in the Public Sphere: Increasingly, ethical firms are actively promoting and supporting the implementation of ethical governance. This entails openly endorsing laws and regulations that advocate for equity, openness, and responsibility. Businesses acknowledge that their lobbying endeavours can influence the establishment of a regulatory framework that is in line with ethical business principles.

Integration of Ethical Principles into Business Models: The incorporation of ethical values into business models is a prominent and noteworthy trend. Businesses are increasingly realising that ethical issues are not just a matter of following rules, but rather a strategic necessity that can improve long-term success. This entails harmonising business models with ethical principles, sustainability objectives, and the welfare of society.

Chapter 2

Social Responsibility of Stakeholders in Corporations

Corporate Social Responsibility (CSR) signifies a significant change in firms' perception and fulfilment of their societal duties. CSR has transformed over the past two decades from a philanthropic idea to a holistic approach that incorporates ethical, social, and environmental factors into fundamental business activities. This essay examines the notion of Corporate Social Responsibility (CSR), tracing its historical evolution, identifying its essential elements, discussing ethical implications, addressing obstacles, and analysing the changing role of businesses in fostering sustainability and social responsibility.

Evolution of Corporate Social Responsibility

The origins of Corporate humanitarian Responsibility may be traced to the early 20th century, during which influential business figures such as Andrew Carnegie and John D. Rockefeller participated in philanthropic endeavours, establishing foundations and providing assistance for humanitarian causes. Nonetheless, the contemporary notion of Corporate Social Responsibility (CSR) started to develop during the 1950s and 1960s in response to mounting apprehensions regarding the ecological and societal consequences of industrialization. Significant literary contributions by authors such as Howard Bowen, who coined the phrase "social responsibility of business," facilitated a more methodical examination of firms' responsibilities to society that extend beyond just profit generation.

Essential Elements of Corporate Social Responsibility

Economic Responsibility: The fundamental aspect of Corporate Social Responsibility (CSR) is economic responsibility, which is the duty of corporations to earn profits and contribute to the advancement of the economy. The CSR perspective prioritises ethical corporate practices, fair competition, and responsible financial management, which deviates from the conventional role of corporations.

Legal responsibilities: Legal responsibility pertains to the obligation of enterprises to comply with both local and international laws and regulations. This encompasses adherence to labour rules, environmental restrictions, consumer protection legislation, and other legal frameworks that dictate business operations.

Ethical responsibilities: Ethical responsibility extends beyond mere adherence to the law, prioritising moral and ethical factors in the process of making decisions. Ethical enterprises place a high value on equity, truthfulness, uprightness, and responsibility when engaging with stakeholders, acknowledging the consequences of their choices on the broader community.

Philanthropic responsibilities: Philanthropic responsibility refers to the act of making voluntary contributions to enhance the overall welfare of society. This encompasses philanthropic contributions, endeavours for local advancement, and backing for societal issues. Philanthropy enables corporations to proactively contribute to tackling societal concerns and promoting beneficial transformation.

Environmental accountability: Given the increasing apprehensions regarding climate change and environmental deterioration, Corporate

Social Responsibility (CSR) has broadened its scope to encompass environmental accountability. Businesses are anticipated to embrace sustainable practices, reduce their ecological impact, and contribute to the conservation of natural resources.

Ethical considerations in corporate social responsibility (CSR)

Transparency and Accountability: Transparency and accountability are essential components of ethical corporate social responsibility (CSR), necessitating openness in both business operations and reporting. Businesses are obligated to take responsibility for their actions, transparently disclosing information about their corporate social responsibility initiatives, and acknowledging any adverse social or environmental consequences.

Stakeholder Engagement: Ethical corporate social responsibility (CSR) entails actively involving a wide array of stakeholders, such as employees, customers, communities, and environmental organisations. Businesses ought to proactively solicit input from stakeholders and take into account their viewpoints in decision-making processes.

Fair Labor Practices: Fair labour standards encompass a crucial aspect of ethical corporate social responsibility (CSR), which entails upholding equitable labour conditions both within the organisation and across the entire supply chain. This entails ensuring the protection of workers' rights, establishing secure working environments, and fostering diversity and inclusivity.

Anti-Corruption Measures: Ethical firms proactively adopt anti-corruption measures, ensuring compliance with ethical standards while engaging with government bodies, rivals, and other stakeholders. Practicing ethical behaviour in business diminishes the likelihood of corruption and promotes a culture characterised by honesty and moral principles.

Responsible Marketing and Advertising: Ethical Corporate Social

Responsibility (CSR) encompasses marketing and advertising techniques. Businesses ought to refrain from engaging in deceptive marketing practices, give utmost importance to honesty in their advertising efforts, and guarantee that their promotional operations are in line with ethical norms.

Obstacles in Executing Corporate Social Responsibility

Balancing Profit Motives and Social Impact: Striking a balance between profit incentives and social impact is a key difficulty when adopting Corporate Social Responsibility (CSR). Businesses may encounter conflicts between the pursuit of shareholder value maximisation and the allocation of resources towards socially responsible endeavours.

Assessing and Communicating Impact: Evaluating the effects of corporate social responsibility (CSR) programmes and effectively communicating these measurements can pose difficulties. It is essential to define precise measures and benchmarks in order to evaluate social and environmental effect accurately. This is necessary for ensuring transparent reporting.

Complex Global Supply networks: In the age of globalisation, companies frequently manage intricate supply networks that extend across numerous nations. Ensuring ethical practices throughout these supply chains, which encompass fair labour conditions and responsible sourcing, poses a substantial challenge.

Short-Term vs. Long-Term Focus: The problem of reconciling short-term financial objectives with long-term sustainability goals is a frequent occurrence. Certain corporate social responsibility (CSR) activities may necessitate an initial investment that yields long-term advantages, thereby generating conflict with short-term profit projections.

Greenwashing and Ethical Washing: Greenwashing, which refers to the act of inflating or making false claims about environmentally beneficial actions, presents a significant obstacle to ethical corporate social responsibility (CSR). In the same vein, several firms partake in ethical washing, when they create an appearance of social responsibility without making any significant commitment.

The Changing Role of Businesses in Corporate Social Responsibility (CSR)

Integration into Business Strategy: A notable development is the incorporation of Corporate Social Responsibility (CSR) into the fundamental business strategy. Nowadays, ethical considerations are regarded as an integral part of long-term success rather than being perceived as separate from business aims.

Innovation for Social Impact: Businesses are progressively utilising innovation to create positive social outcomes. This encompasses the creation of environmentally sustainable products, the use of eco-friendly technologies, and active participation in addressing societal issues.

International Cooperation for Sustainable Objectives:

Businesses are engaging in global collaboration to tackle interconnected global challenges, including climate change, poverty, and inequality. Collaborations among enterprises, non-profit organisations, and governments are promoting joint efforts towards sustainable development.

Emphasising Diversity, Equity, and Inclusion: Ethical firms are prioritising diversity, equity, and inclusion. In response to the recognition of their social obligation to address systematic disparities, corporations are adopting policies aimed at fostering diversity in both the workplace and other areas.

Technology for Social Good: Utilising technology for the betterment of society is a current focus of attention. Enterprises are leveraging technology to develop inventive remedies for societal issues, ranging from mitigating healthcare inequalities to enhancing educational accessibility.

Community engagement and empowerment: Businesses are proactively involving themselves in local communities, attentively listening to their needs, and empowering them through corporate social responsibility (CSR) activities. This entails engaging in partnerships with community organisations, providing assistance to education and healthcare initiatives, and making contributions towards the promotion of sustainable development.

Corporate Social Responsibility signifies a fundamental change in the way businesses understand their role in society. CSR, or Corporate Social Responsibility, has evolved from its charitable origins to a complete strategy that includes economic, legal, ethical, philanthropic, and environmental duties. It now serves as a guiding framework for businesses to conduct themselves ethically.

When organisations deal with the ethical aspects of Corporate Social Responsibility (CSR), they face issues such as finding a balance between profit goals, quantifying the effects of their actions, and managing intricate global supply chains. These challenges require careful and well-thought-out solutions. The changing role of firms in corporate social responsibility (CSR) reflects a wider movement towards incorporating ethical practices into fundamental business objectives, utilising innovation to create social benefits, and engaging in global collaborations to tackle common concerns.

Ultimately, it is essential for firms to adopt Corporate Social Responsibility not only as a moral duty but also as a crucial strategic requirement. Businesses that give priority to ethical considerations not only contribute to the well-being of society, but also position themselves for long-term success in a world that is becoming more conscientious and linked. The changing nature of corporate social responsibility highlights the significant capacity of corporations to act as catalysts for beneficial transformation within society.

Comprehensive investigation: social responsibilities of business stakeholders

Enterprises function within a complex web of interactions that involve a wide variety of stakeholders, each of whom plays a distinct role in the achievement of the enterprise's goals and the maintenance of its operation. It is important to note that the social duties of business stakeholders, which include owners, employees, customers, and the community, are complex and intertwined throughout the firm. The social duties of each stakeholder group are investigated in depth in this essay. The roles, ethical considerations, and contributions that each stakeholder group makes to a socially responsible business environment are also discussed.

I. The Financial and Social Obligations of Owners:

Economic responsibilities: It is the obligation of the owners to ensure that the company is financially viable and profitable. This responsibility falls under the category of economic responsibility. Making strategic decisions, effectively allocating resources, and cultivating an environment that is conducive to the expansion of a corporation are all required steps in this process. The fulfilment of financial duties to employees, suppliers, and other stakeholders is that which is included in the concept of economic responsibility.

Legal Responsibility: Owners are burdened with legal responsibilities, which include ensuring that the business works within the framework of applicable laws and regulations. Compliance with tax laws, labour laws, environmental rules, and industry-specific requirements are all included in this category. The commitment to respecting legal standards and fostering a culture of compliance inside the organisation is an essential component of ethical ownership.

Ethical responsibilities: Ethical duty Integrity in financial dealings, transparency in decision-making, and a dedication to ethical business practices are all components of the ethical duty that owners are expected to uphold. Owners should make fairness, honesty, and accountability their top priorities in all of their interactions, whether they are with internal stakeholders or with stakeholders from outside the organisation. Ethical leadership is the foundation upon which the entire organisation is built.

Employee Welfare and Development: The welfare and development of employees is a social obligation that owners have, and they are responsible for the well-being and growth of their employees. The provision of equitable salaries, the guarantee of secure working conditions, and the encouragement of possibilities for professional development are all included in this. It is also important to develop a positive culture in the workplace that encourages diversity, inclusiveness, and equitable chances for all employees. This is an extension of ethical ownership.

Philanthropy and Community Engagement: The concept of philanthropic duty for owners entails making contributions to the general welfare of society by way of charitable donations, community development initiatives, and support for social causes. The philanthropic part of owners' social duties is reflected in their engagement with local communities, their understanding of the needs of such communities, and their active contribution to the development of those communities.

II. Social Responsibilities of Employees:

Productivity and Performance: Employees play a crucial role in fulfilling the economic obligations of the firm by maintaining optimal levels of productivity and performance. Employees have a social responsibility to meet their work tasks, achieve goals, and consistently enhance their individual and collective performance.

Ethical Work Practices: Employees have an ethical responsibility to follow ethical work practices, uphold organisational values, and foster a culture of integrity. Employees are accountable for engaging in transparent communication, equitable treatment of peers, and principled decision-making within their professional capacities.

Professional Development: Employees have a moral obligation to actively pursue their own professional growth. Proactively pursuing chances to improve skills, staying updated on industry trends, and consistently enhancing expertise all contribute to the overall growth and profitability of the organisation.

Workplace Collaboration and Inclusion: It is the employees' duty to cultivate a workplace culture that promotes collaboration and inclusivity. This entails demonstrating respect towards coworkers, embracing diversity, and actively engaging in the creation of a work environment that is both positive and inclusive.

Corporate Citizenship: Employees fulfil the philanthropic obligations of the company by engaging in corporate citizenship. This may entail engaging in community service projects, taking part in corporate social responsibility activities, and actively endorsing philanthropic endeavours that are in line with the company's principles.

III. Social Responsibilities of Consumers:

Rational Decision-Making: Consumers bear a societal obligation to make well-informed purchasing choices. This entails conducting product research, comprehending their ecological and societal repercussions, and selecting brands that adhere to ethical and sustainable principles.

Promoting Ethical Businesses: Consumers uphold ethical duty by endorsing businesses that prioritise ethical and sustainable operations. Opting for products and services offered by socially responsible enterprises promotes a transition in the market towards sustainability and ethical business practices.

Feedback and Advocacy: Consumers are obligated to offer feedback to firms regarding their products and practices. Expressing apprehensions, commending moral endeavours, and promoting sustainable methodologies all help to generating a need for socially conscientious products and services.

Waste Reduction and Responsible Consumption: Consumers play a crucial part in environmental stewardship by actively minimising waste and adopting responsible consumption habits. This encompasses the reduction of single-use plastic, the practice of recycling, and the selection of options that are in line with sustainability objectives.

Social Engagement: Consumers have the opportunity to actively participate in awareness campaigns, lend their support to social causes, and utilise their power to persuade firms to embrace responsible practices. Consumers who actively participate in social issues help to the development of a culture that emphasises the ethical obligations of corporations.

IV. Social Obligations of the Community:

Economic Development: The community bears a social obligation to contribute to the advancement of the economy. Engaging in the patronage of local businesses, fostering entrepreneurial endeavours, and actively participating in economic endeavours are all factors that enhance the general welfare of the community.

Environmental management is a collective duty that communities must share. This entails actively engaging in efforts to safeguard natural resources, mitigate pollution, and tackle environmental issues that affect the well-being of the community.

Education and awareness are promoted by communities as part of their social obligation. This encompasses endorsing educational endeavours, distributing knowledge regarding social and environmental concerns, and cultivating a climate of intellectual growth within the community.

Engagement with Businesses: Communities can engage with businesses to tackle common obstacles and advocate for ethical practices. Interacting with businesses, actively engaging in community development activities, and offering feedback all foster a mutually beneficial relationship between businesses and communities.

Social inclusion and support: Communities bear the need to cultivate social inclusion and provide assistance to disadvantaged or marginalised groups within the community. This entails fostering diversity, championing for equitable opportunities, and establishing an inclusive atmosphere that safeguards the welfare of all individuals within the community.

Community Development Initiatives: Engaging actively in community development initiatives is a social obligation that communities can accomplish. This encompasses working together with local organisations, providing assistance to infrastructure projects, and engaging in efforts that improve the overall standard of living in the community.

Advocacy for Social Causes: Social concerns can be advocated for by communities that share the same values and priorities. This entails garnering backing for causes such as social equity, ecological preservation, and other concerns that affect the welfare of the community and beyond.

Ethical considerations pertaining to various stakeholders

Transparency and accountability: Transparency and accountability are essential ethical principles that apply to all individuals and groups involved. It is essential for owners, employees, consumers, and the community to give utmost importance to transparent communication, truthful disclosure, and accountability for their activities.

Equity and parity: Equity and parity are essential moral standards that ought to govern the conduct of all parties involved. Promoting equitable treatment, equal access to opportunities, and the absence of prejudice are essential for fostering an ethical and socially conscious company environment.

Environmental consciousness: Consciousness related to environment is an integral part of ethical duty. Businesses, employees, consumers, and communities ought to take into account the ecological consequences of their actions and embrace strategies that encourage sustainability and conscientious resource management.

Social Justice and Inclusion: Social justice and inclusivity are fundamental ethical principles. Stakeholders should proactively strive to eradicate discrimination, foster inclusivity, and provide equitable opportunities and representation for all individuals, irrespective of their backgrounds.

Chapter 3

The Response of Indian Firms to wards Corporate Social Responsibility (CSR)

The progression of Corporate Social Responsibility (CSR) in Indian companies:

Throughout history, Indian culture has deeply embedded philanthropy and humanitarian endeavours, which in turn have shaped the corporate social responsibility (CSR) environment. Nevertheless, the systematic incorporation of Corporate Social Responsibility (CSR) into company activities received impetus with the enactment of the Companies Act in 2013. This legislation required specific eligible corporations to allocate a part of their earnings towards corporate social responsibility (CSR) initiatives, indicating a significant change in how businesses perceived their obligations to society.

Regulatory Structure:

The implementation of the Companies Act, 2013, was a significant turning point for Corporate Social Responsibility (CSR) in India. According to the law, corporations that meet certain requirements are required to allocate a minimum of 2% of their average net income from the past three years to corporate social responsibility (CSR) activities. The implementation of this regulatory framework introduced a systematic approach to corporate social responsibility (CSR) efforts, mandating eligible enterprises to comply and demonstrating the government's dedication to promoting ethical business conduct.

Notable Corporate Social Responsibility (CSR) endeavours undertaken by Indian companies

Education and Skill Development: Numerous Indian companies have prioritised projects related to education and skill development. Companies are forming partnerships with educational institutions, establishing skill development centres, and financing educational programmes to improve the ability of individuals to find employment and contribute to the development of human capital.

Healthcare and sanitation: Healthcare and sanitation have been focal points for corporate social responsibility (CSR) endeavours. Companies are allocating resources towards the development of healthcare infrastructure, facilitating medical research, and implementing health awareness initiatives. In addition, endeavours are being undertaken to ensure access to sanitary facilities and encourage cleanliness practices.

Sustainability: Environmental sustainability is becoming an increasingly important area of concern for Indian companies. Initiatives encompass afforestation projects, waste management programmes, and the adoption of environmentally sustainable practices. Businesses are progressively acknowledging the significance of diminishing their ecological impact.

Community development: Development of communities continues to be a prominent focus in corporate social responsibility (CSR) initiatives. Companies are actively engaged in community endeavours, such as constructing infrastructure, promoting rural advancement, and empowering marginalised groups through diverse social and economic endeavours.

Encouraging Entrepreneurship: Certain companies are actively promoting economic growth by nurturing entrepreneurship. This entails delivering help to small and medium enterprises (SMEs), providing financial aid, and promoting skill enhancement initiatives to empower local entrepreneurs.

Obstacles Encountered by Indian Companies in Executing Corporate Social Responsibility (CSR) Initiatives

Strategic Alignment: Some organisations still face difficulties in aligning their CSR initiatives with their fundamental business strategy. Strategically integrating thorough planning is necessary to achieve a balance between societal impact and commercial aims.

Measuring Impact: Evaluating the concrete effects of corporate social responsibility (CSR) initiatives presents a difficulty. Many companies face challenges in defining precise measures to evaluate the efficacy of their activities and to showcase the value generated for both society and the business.

Compliance and reporting: It involve the intricate task of adhering to regulatory requirements and ensuring clear and transparent reporting. Certain companies encounter difficulties in manoeuvring between the legal obligations and effectively conveying their corporate social responsibility initiatives to stakeholders.

Resource Allocation: Effectively allocating resources for corporate social responsibility (CSR) programmes while maintaining economic viability is a prevalent concern. Strategically managing financial obligations to corporate social responsibility (CSR) alongside other operational requirements necessitates meticulous financial strategizing.

Establishing enduring transformation: Attaining sustainable and enduring transformation in societal matters remains an ongoing obstacle.

While several corporate social responsibility (CSR) efforts prioritise short-term effects, achieving systemic reforms that tackle underlying issues necessitates sustained dedication and cooperation.

The influence of Corporate Social Responsibility (CSR) on Indian companies and society:

Improved business Reputation: Companies who actively participate in Corporate Social Responsibility (CSR) initiatives have observed an increased business reputation. Engaging in socially responsible practices fosters trust among consumers, investors, and the broader community, thereby enhancing brand perception.

Employee engagement and retention: these two factors are positively influenced by corporate social responsibility (CSR) efforts. Workers are increasingly looking for significance and intention in their profession, and a company's dedication to social responsibility can improve workplace contentment and allegiance.

Stakeholder relationships: Companies that actively engage in corporate social responsibility (CSR) programmes have enhanced their relationships with diverse stakeholders, such as government entities, local communities, and non-governmental organisations (NGOs). This cooperative approach cultivates a favourable corporate atmosphere.

Innovation and Sustainability: CSR efforts foster innovation and promote sustainability among companies. Companies that embrace responsible practices are more inclined to incorporate environmental and social factors into their business strategies, resulting in enduring sustainability.

Social Impact: Arguably, the most notable consequence is the constructive transformation that occurs inside society. CSR activities have made significant contributions to enhancing education, healthcare, environmental preservation, and community development, thereby exerting a positive impact on the lives of numerous individuals.

To conclude, The reaction of Indian companies to corporate social responsibility (CSR) demonstrates a dynamic and ever-changing environment. The Companies Act, 2013, has been instrumental in establishing and organising CSR practices through regulatory measures. Companies are progressively acknowledging the significance of matching their corporate goals with the demands of society, so promoting a more sustainable and socially responsible business environment.

Despite ongoing obstacles, the influence of corporate social responsibility (CSR) activities on both businesses and society is clearly apparent. In addition to adhering to legal requirements, Indian companies are actively adopting their social obligations, promoting beneficial transformation, and making significant contributions to the comprehensive advancement of the country. In order to tackle urgent societal issues and create a more inclusive and sustainable future, it is crucial for corporations, government, and civil society to work together in the ever-changing CSR landscape.

Chapter 4

Social Responsibility and Safeguarding Consumers

Corporate Social Responsibility (CSR) and consumer protection are essential components of contemporary business strategies, with the goal of promoting enduring and morally upright connections between corporations and their stakeholders. Corporate Social Responsibility (CSR) refers to a company's dedication to making a good impact on society that goes beyond its financial objectives. Conversely, consumer protection guarantees equitable treatment and provision of precise information to consumers, so fostering transparency and confidence.

CSR programmes involve multiple aspects, including environmental sustainability, charity, ethical labour practices, and community engagement. Companies can reduce their ecological impact and address concerns about climate change and resource depletion by implementing environmentally friendly strategies. Engaging in philanthropic endeavours, such as providing financial assistance to education or healthcare initiatives, positively impact the overall welfare of society, while simultaneously bolstering a company's reputation and brand image.

CSR encompasses ethical labour practices that encompass equitable remuneration, secure working environments, and unbiased opportunity for all personnel. Promoting a workforce that is diverse and inclusive not only reflects society ideals, but also fosters a more inventive and adaptive organisation. Community engagement, a component of corporate social responsibility (CSR), is firms actively interacting in local communities to tackle social issues and establish partnerships that go beyond transactional interactions.

Consumer protection is a supplementary element that ensures the rights and interests of consumers are protected. Consumer protection encompasses the essential components of precise product details, equitable pricing, and the preservation of private rights. Regulations and oversight organisations have a vital function in ensuring compliance with these norms, by holding firms responsible for their ethical behaviour.

Companies that place a high importance on corporate social responsibility (CSR) and safeguarding consumer interests have a tendency to establish enduring trust with their customers. An open and accountable approach cultivates loyalty and favourable consumer opinions. Conversely, occurrences of immoral conduct or disregarding consumer rights can result in harm to one's reputation and negative financial consequences.

As customers become more knowledgeable and aware of social and environmental concerns, corporations are acknowledging the significance of incorporating corporate social responsibility (CSR) and consumer protection into their fundamental strategies. By aligning business processes with ethical and sustainable principles, firms not only fulfil regulatory requirements but also establish themselves as responsible corporate citizens in the eyes of their customers.

The relationship between corporate social responsibility (CSR) and consumer protection in promoting ethical corporate conduct:

The interdependence between Corporate Social Responsibility (CSR) and consumer protection is a fundamental aspect in promoting ethical corporate conduct. These two factors have a reciprocal effect, forming a mutually beneficial relationship that not only advantages enterprises but also enhances the overall welfare of society.

Transparency and Trust: Corporate Social Responsibility (CSR) programmes frequently encompass corporate practices that are characterised by transparency, such supplier chain transparency and the publication of environmental impact assessments. The transparency is intricately connected to safeguarding consumer interests, guaranteeing that consumers are provided with precise and reliable information regarding products and services. When consumers have confidence in a company's dedication to CSR principles, it lays the groundwork for an open and reliable relationship.

Ethical Consumer Choices: Consumer protection guarantees that consumers are provided with accurate information to make well-informed decisions on their purchases. Companies that adopt CSR generally conform their processes to ethical standards, enabling consumers to choose choices that line with their values. Increased consciousness of ethical consumerism serves as a motivating factor, compelling corporations to embrace responsible practices in order to fulfil customer demands.

Reputation and Brand Image: Corporate Social Responsibility (CSR) efforts make a substantial contribution to fostering a favourable brand image. Engaging in actions that help society, such as supporting social causes or implementing sustainable practices, increases a company's reputation. A favourable brand image, in turn, serves as a means of safeguarding consumers, since they are more inclined to select items from companies renowned for their ethical conduct.

Customer loyalty over an extended period: The establishment of trust and a favourable reputation through corporate social responsibility programmes has a direct impact on customer loyalty. Consumer loyalty to a brand is more likely to be maintained when they perceive that the company genuinely prioritises social and environmental concerns. The enduring loyalty serves as a means of safeguarding the company against abrupt changes in consumer perception, thereby providing consumer protection.

Regulatory Compliance: Both Corporate Social Responsibility (CSR) and consumer protection are governed by regulatory frameworks. Companies that actively participate in corporate social responsibility (CSR) initiatives frequently discover that they naturally conform to consumer protection rules. Adhering to ethical company practices, implementing fair pricing strategies, and maintaining honest communication not only benefit consumers but also guarantee adherence to legal regulations, thereby mitigating the likelihood of legal repercussions.

Social Licence to Operate: Corporate Social Responsibility (CSR) efforts extend beyond mere compliance with legal obligations; they actively contribute to a company's social licence to operate. Corporate acceptance and approval refers to the recognition and endorsement that a firm receives from the communities and stakeholders it engages with. The concept of consumer protection is intrinsically intertwined with this idea, as corporations must abide by ethical norms in order to uphold a favourable connection with their wider community.

Companies that have a strong connection between corporate social responsibility (CSR) and consumer protection are better equipped to adjust to shifting market trends. Companies that adopt corporate social responsibility (CSR) practices are in a better position to comply with the evolving consumer desires for sustainable and ethical products. This adaptability serves as a means of safeguarding enterprises from becoming obsolete in a dynamic market, therefore functioning as a type of consumer protection.

How CSR and consumer protection promote consumer trust:

Transparency, ethics, and a commitment to social well-being help CSR and consumer protection companies develop consumer trust. These companies build and sustain trust:

Communicating Openly: Transparency about business practices, principles, and CSR promotes trust. Clear communication about product origin, manufacturing, and environmental implications helps consumers choose.

Ethics in Business: Ethical companies build trust through fair labour and appropriate sourcing. Customers trust firms that care about their workers and the communities they serve.

Value-Based CSR: CSR projects that match consumers' values establish a strong bond. Customers that care about social issues and the environment like companies that support them. This alignment increases the company-customer emotional tie.

Consistency in Action: Integrity between a company's values and actions is key. When corporations continuously practise CSR and consumer protection, people trust them. Deviations from values swiftly destroy confidence.

Being accountable and responsive: Take responsibility for mistakes, resolve issues quickly, and address consumer complaints to establish confidence. Accountability, correction, and learning from mistakes build trust in companies.

Consumer Engagement and Feedback: Engaging consumers and soliciting feedback builds trust. Companies that listen to customers, implement feedback into their strategy, and genuinely care about their needs build trust and transparency.

Transparency on social media: Active social media involvement lets companies reach consumers directly. Sharing behind-the-scenes information, CSR updates, and open responses build trust.

Credentials and Verification: Displaying ethical, sustainability, or consumer protection certifications provides external validation. Third-party endorsements boost consumer trust in a company's ethics.

Long-term CSR commitment: Over time, companies that commit to CSR long-term establish confidence. Consumers value long-term initiatives beyond marketing.

Initiatives in education: Customers are better informed by companies that explain their CSR activities, industry difficulties, and consumer choices. Educated consumers trust knowledge-based companies.

Measurable impact and reporting: Regular reporting on CSR efforts and evidence of its impact generate trust. Transparently reporting environmental and social results boosts a company's credibility.

Unethical functional management issues

Unethical dilemmas can emerge in several operational domains of management, affecting areas such as sales, marketing, and technology. It is imperative to identify and resolve these challenges in order to uphold ethical standards within an organisation. Below are several prevalent ethical considerations within each functional domain:

1. Sales:

Fraudulent and Dishonest Practices: Sales agents may participate in deception through the act of embellishing product attributes or disseminating false assertions regarding competitors. Engaging in deceitful tactics undermines confidence and may result in legal ramifications.

Aggressive sales techniques and manipulative strategies: Engaging in coercive tactics to induce clients to make unnecessary purchases or employing manipulative strategies to exploit susceptible persons are examples of unethical sales practices. These actions prioritise immediate profits over the welfare of customers.

Corruption and Illicit Payments: The act of providing or receiving bribes, kickbacks, or other forms of incentives in order to obtain deals or obtain preferential treatment can undermine the integrity of sales procedures.

2. Marketing:

Deceptive Advertising: Engaging in deceptive advertising by making inaccurate or deceptive statements about products or services can lead to consumer misinformation and the formation of unrealistic expectations. This behaviour erodes consumer confidence and has the potential to result in regulatory complications.

Deceptive Advertising Strategies: Utilising manipulative strategies, such as emotional manipulation or capitalising on cognitive biases, to shape consumer behaviour is morally wrong. It weakens the independence of consumers and can result in unfortunate buying choices.

Instances of breaches in personal privacy: Unethical marketing techniques encompass the unauthorised acquisition or utilisation of consumer data, so infringing upon privacy rights. The issue of unauthorised targeted advertising is becoming increasingly worrisome in the era of digital technology.

3. Technology:

Data Privacy Breaches: The unauthorised entry, improper use, or mismanagement of user data constitutes a substantial ethical concern. Data breaches undermine the confidentiality of individuals and diminish confidence in technological firms.

Algorithmic bias: It refers to the phenomenon when algorithms exhibit unfair or discriminatory behaviour against certain individuals or groups due to inherent biases in the data or design of the algorithm.

Unconscious prejudice during the construction of algorithms or AI systems can lead to discriminatory results. This prejudice has the potential to have a greater impact on some groups, which raises ethical considerations in the context of technology applications.

Instances of infringement on intellectual property: Engaging in unauthorised use or replication of intellectual property, such as engaging in software piracy or infringing on patents, is an unethical behaviour that diminishes the worth of innovation and creativity.

4. Human Resources:

Issues of discrimination and harassment: Unfair recruiting practices, workplace harassment, or preferential treatment based on personal connections rather than qualifications are morally wrong and can result in a harmful work atmosphere.

Violation of labour laws: Exploitative labour practices, such as insufficient remuneration, hazardous work environments, or contravention of labour regulations, pose substantial ethical dilemmas in the administration of human resources.

5. Finance:

Fraudulent activities in the financial sector: Financial fraud include activities such as manipulating financial records, engaging in insider trading, or disseminating inaccurate financial information to stakeholders, all of which undermine the integrity of financial management.

Conflict of interest: Non-disclosure and neglect of conflicts of interest in financial decision-making can result in biassed decision-making and erode the trust of investors and stakeholders.

To tackle these immoral concerns, it is imperative to demonstrate a steadfast dedication to ethical leadership, establish unambiguous organisational principles, and provide continuous training for personnel. Companies that place ethical issues at the forefront of all parts of management are more inclined to establish trust, cultivate long-term partnerships, and uphold a positive reputation in the marketplace.

CSR and competitive strategy

Competitive strategy within the framework of Corporate Social Responsibility (CSR) is incorporating ethical and socially responsible activities into a company's comprehensive business plan in order to attain a competitive edge. Companies integrate CSR with their fundamental business aims rather than seeing it as a distinct endeavour. Below are the primary factors to consider and advantages of integrating Corporate Social Responsibility (CSR) into a competitive strategy:

1. Brand Differentiation: Corporate Social Responsibility (CSR) enables organisations to set themselves apart from competitors by showcasing their dedication to social and environmental initiatives. Consumers are showing a growing preference for brands that have a positive impact, which makes corporate social responsibility (CSR) a potent tool for distinguishing one company from another.

2. Consumer Trust and Loyalty: Companies that give priority to Corporate Social Responsibility (CSR) establish a strong bond of trust with their consumers. Consumers are more likely to be loyal to businesses that share their values, as a result of their strong ethical stance and responsible activities. This level of trust has the potential to result in enduring consumer relationships.

3. Staff Engagement and Talent Attraction: Adhering to CSR can bolster staff morale and foster greater engagement. Employees frequently experience a sense of pride when working for socially responsible organisations, resulting in increased job satisfaction and reduced employee turnover. Furthermore, socially responsible practices have the ability to attract highly skilled individuals who are seeking settings that prioritise a sense of purpose.

4. Risk Management: Incorporating CSR into competitive strategy requires taking proactive measures to mitigate risks. Organisations that actively manage social and environmental risks, such as challenges in their supply chain or negative environmental effects, are more equipped to effectively manage crises and protect their reputation.

5. Cost Efficiency and Innovation: Corporate Social Responsibility (CSR) can enhance operational efficiency by promoting sustainable practices. Companies that implement waste reduction strategies, optimise energy efficiency, and adopt environmentally friendly practices frequently discover financial benefits. Moreover, placing emphasis on Corporate Social Responsibility (CSR) can serve as a catalyst for innovation, as organisations actively pursue sustainable approaches to address their business obstacles.

6. Capital Accessibility: Investors are progressively taking into account environmental, social, and governance (ESG) aspects when determining their investment choices. Companies that have strong corporate social responsibility (CSR) procedures may have an advantage in attracting funds, as they align with the increasing trend of socially responsible investing.

7. Community Relations and Market Access: Participating in corporate social responsibility (CSR) programmes enhances connections with nearby communities. Companies that actively contribute to the well-being of the community receive local support, which helps them enter the market more easily and reduces potential opposition.

8. Regulatory Compliance: CSR ensures that organisations adhere to changing regulatory standards, enabling them to remain ahead of compliance responsibilities. Taking proactive measures to resolve social and environmental issues mitigates the likelihood of encountering legal complications and regulatory penalties.

9. Collaboration and Partnerships: Companies dedicated to Corporate Social Responsibility (CSR) may discover prospects for collaboration with similar organisations. Establishing collaborations for social impact can result in cooperative endeavours that yield advantages for both the participating companies and the broader community.

Incorporating corporate social responsibility (CSR) into competitive strategy extends beyond simple acts of altruism; it becomes a strategic need for organisations seeking to flourish in a socially aware market. Companies that prioritise Corporate Social Responsibility (CSR) not only contribute to positive societal results but also establish themselves as frontrunners in an era where ethical considerations significantly impact consumer and investor choices.

Chapter 5

Cost Benefit Analysis

Corporate social responsibility (CSR) cost-benefit analyses (CBAs) look at the monetary and non-monetary effects of CSR programmes to see if they're worth it. Companies understand that ethical activities help them stay competitive and sustainable in the long run, even if the benefits of CSR are difficult to pin down and frequently involve multiple factors. In this part, we will examine the cost-benefit analysis:

Costs:

Implementation costs: Sustainable practices, ethical sourcing, and staff training are all examples of CSR activities that might have hefty initial expenses. Among these investments are those in human capital, physical facilities, and technological advancements.

Legal costs: There can be extra expenses to pay to meet industry standards and regulatory regulations. Investing in ESG (environmental, social, and governance) compliance is essential for companies.

Costs for Reporting and Tracking: There would be administrative costs associated with tracking and reporting on CSR performance on a regular basis. Preparing sustainability reports, audits, and metric tracking are all part of this process to guarantee openness.

The Risk of Decreased Revenue: A temporary drop in income or profit could be the outcome of certain CSR projects, particularly if the business abandons less sustainable but more lucrative activities.

Positive aspects

Improved Brand Recognition and Reputation: A better reputation for the business might be the outcome of CSR initiatives that boost the company's public perception. Consequently, this has the potential to draw in a larger pool of socially conscious consumers, investors, and partners.

Boosted Revenue and Customer Loyalty: A company's ethical standards are becoming more and more of a factor for consumers when making purchasing decisions. An boost in sales and brand loyalty can more than cover the costs of implementing a CSR effort if it strikes a chord with consumers.

Motivation and Efficiency in the Workplace: A decrease in employee turnover and an increase in production are both outcomes of engaged and motivated workers. Better employee engagement and output can result from corporate social responsibility (CSR) programmes that put an emphasis on diversity, inclusion, and health and wellness.

Taking Precautions: Companies can minimise the impact of unfavourable events by identifying and addressing potential risks early on through CSR. The organisation can avoid possible financial losses by reducing legal, regulatory, and reputational risks through proactive risk management.

Confidence among Investors and Availability of Capital: When making investing decisions, more and more investors are taking ESG aspects into account. Capital may be more easily obtained, borrowing costs reduced, and investor trust boosted by companies with robust CSR procedures.

Efficient Operations and Financial Benefits: Adopting sustainable and efficient techniques is a common component of CSR projects. In the long run, businesses might save money by cutting down on energy use, trash, and resource usage.

Distinctiveness in the Market and Innovation: As businesses look for long-term solutions, CSR initiatives encourage new ideas. A brand can gain an edge in the market by standing out from the crowd with creative and socially conscious products and services.

Connections with Stakeholders and the Community: Businesses may run more smoothly, with less resistance, if they cultivate positive relationships with local communities and stakeholders. on sectors that have a significant influence on the immediate area, this can be quite useful.

Analysing in Balance: A company's capacity to find a middle ground between immediate expenses and potential returns is crucial to the success of any CSR cost-benefit analysis. Improved reputation is one of those perks that might not pay off right away, but it adds up to a lot of value for the business in the long run.

To sum up, corporate social responsibility (CSR) projects do have initial expenses, but they can pay off in the long run with tangible and intangible advantages that can boost a company's success. Corporate social responsibility (CSR) cost-benefit analyses indicate that ethical business practices are an investment in long-term growth and competitiveness as well as a responsibility of corporations.

4.1 Calculating cost-benefit analysis

Conducting a cost-benefit analysis (CBA) for Corporate Social Responsibility (CSR) entails evaluating the monetary and non-monetary effects of CSR efforts. Below is a comprehensive structure to assist you in navigating the computation process:

1. Determine expenses:

A. Implementation Costs : - Calculate the total expenditures related to the execution of corporate social responsibility activities. This encompasses expenses related to technology, infrastructure, personnel training, and any other necessary investments.

B. Compliance Costs : - Determine expenses associated with adhering to regulatory mandates and industry benchmarks. These charges may include costs for obtaining certifications, conducting audits, and making necessary revisions to comply with ESG requirements.

C. Reporting and Monitoring Costs : - Determine the expenditures related to the routine monitoring, reporting, and recording of corporate social responsibility (CSR) performance. This encompasses the expenses associated with monitoring performance indicators, performing examinations, and compiling sustainability documentation.

D. Potential income Loss : - Evaluate any immediate decline in income or profit resulting from corporate social responsibility programmes, particularly when shifting away from less environmentally friendly practices.

2. Determine the advantages:

A. Improved Reputation and Brand Image: - Measure the influence of a favourable corporate image on consumer perceptions, loyalty, and the potential for increased sales.

B. Customer Loyalty and greater Sales : - Calculate the financial gains coming from enhanced customer loyalty and greater sales as a direct consequence of corporate social responsibility (CSR) efforts.

C. Employee Engagement and Productivity : - Assess the influence of enhanced employee engagement on productivity, perhaps leading to a decrease in recruiting and training expenses.

D. Risk Mitigation : - Assess the possible cost reductions resulting from the prevention or reduction of legal, regulatory, and reputational concerns through proactive corporate social responsibility initiatives.

E. Access to Capital and Investor Confidence : - Evaluate the economic advantages, such as reduced borrowing expenses or heightened market valuation, that arise from improved access to funds and bolstered investor trust.

F. Operational Efficiency and Cost Savings : - Measure the monetary benefits derived from implementing more effective and environmentally friendly operational procedures, such as decreased energy usage and waste generation.

G. Innovation and Market Differentiation : - Assess the possible financial advantages derived from innovative corporate social responsibility (CSR) initiatives, such as the development of unique products or services, which could result in a larger market share or higher prices.

H. Community and Stakeholder Relations : - Evaluate the significance of cultivating favourable connections with nearby communities and stakeholders in relation to streamlining operations and mitigating resistance.

3. Analyse the expenses and advantages:

A. Monetary Quantification : - Translate all costs and benefits into monetary values to facilitate comparison. This may entail approximating values through market research, historical data, or expert judgements.

B. Timeframe: - Evaluate the duration during which costs and benefits will be experienced. Long-term benefits, such as improved reputation, can be gained, but certain upfront expenditures may be incurred.

C. Discounting : - Utilise discount rates to adjust future expenses and benefits in order to consider the monetary value of time. This facilitates the comparison of costs and benefits that arise at distinct time intervals.

D. Net Present Value (NPV) : - Compute the Net Present Value by deducting the aggregate expenses from the aggregate benefits. A positive net present value (NPV) signifies that the advantages surpass the expenses.

E. Return on Investment (ROI) : - Calculate the ROI by dividing the net benefits by the total costs and representing it as a percentage. A positive return on investment (ROI) signifies a beneficial outcome in relation to the initial investment.

4. Qualitative variables:

Take into account non-financial or qualitative variables that contribute to the total influence of Corporate Social Responsibility (CSR). These may encompass enhanced organisational culture, fortified stakeholder alliances, or favourable ecological and societal effects.

5. Cognitive Process of Making Choices:

Make a well-informed decision by considering the calculated net benefits, return on investment (ROI), and qualitative factors. Assess whether the monetary and non-monetary benefits are in accordance with the objectives and principles of the organisation.

It is important to keep in mind that the precision of estimates can differ depending on the data available, assumptions made, and the level of complexity of corporate social responsibility efforts. Regularly evaluating and revising the analysis is crucial as the organisation develops and new information emerges.

Chapter 6

Broader Social Responsibility

Corporate Social Responsibility (CSR) extends beyond national limitations and acknowledges the interdependence of the global business landscape. Global companies are required to use responsible business practices that promote good social impact and environmental sustainability worldwide. Corporate Social Responsibility (CSR) encompasses the dedication of corporations to make beneficial contributions to society and the environment, alongside their pursuit of economic prosperity, on a worldwide scale. It acknowledges that firms work in a globalised world with interconnected social, economic, and environmental concerns, which go beyond local or national boundaries. These are the fundamental elements of Corporate Social Responsibility (CSR) in this particular context:

I. Corporate citizenship

Effective corporate citizenship entails corporations meeting their social and ethical responsibilities while also acknowledging the significance of enduring viability and achievement. The following are fundamental elements that characterise strong corporate citizenship:

Societal and ethical responsibilities: Principles of integrity in business: Conducting business with integrity, honesty, and fairness in all transactions. Abiding by ethical principles is essential for demonstrating excellent corporate citizenship.

Effective Corporate Governance: Enacting governance mechanisms that are both transparent and responsible, with a focus on prioritising the interests of stakeholders like as shareholders, employees, consumers, and the broader community.

Employee well-being: Placing a high importance on the welfare and equitable treatment of employees. This encompasses ensuring a secure and conducive working atmosphere, equitable remuneration, avenues for career advancement, and a dedication to fostering diversity and inclusivity.

Ecological Responsibility: Implementing sustainable measures aimed at minimising adverse environmental effects. This entails the prudent use of resources, the mitigation of carbon emissions, and the active participation in ecological preservation.

Participation and involvement of the community: Engaging in and making valuable contributions to the welfare of nearby communities. This may entail providing assistance to education, healthcare, and community development endeavours.

Charitable giving: Participating in philanthropic endeavours, such as making charity contributions or forming alliances with nonprofit organisations, in order to tackle social problems and enhance societal well-being.

Supplier and partner relationships: Ensuring equitable and morally upright behaviours across the whole supply chain. This entails advocating for ethical sourcing and fostering partnerships with suppliers and collaborators who uphold comparable principles.

Customer Relations: Ensuring equitable treatment of customers, delivering precise information regarding products and services, and rapidly resolving customer inquiries. Establishing trust through open and morally upright relationships is of utmost importance.

Endurance and Achievement in the Long Run

Integration of Corporate Social Responsibility (CSR) in a strategic manner:
Incorporating corporate social responsibility (CSR) into the fundamental business strategy. Ensuring the alignment of corporate social responsibility (CSR) programmes with the company's values and objectives guarantees the sustainability and long-term profitability of the organisation.

Advancing Sustainable Solutions through Innovation: Promoting the cultivation of inventive ideas to create economically feasible and ecologically sustainable products, services, and business models. Striking a balance between profitability and environmental and social factors is crucial.

Flexibility in response to changes in market trends: Remaining aware of changing consumer tastes and cultural expectations. Modifying corporate strategies to conform with evolving market trends, such as an increasing desire for socially conscious products and services.

Hazard Mitigation: Anticipating and resolving potential risks in a proactive manner, encompassing issues related to reputation, regulations, and operations. Efficiently mitigating risks enhances the company's enduring ability to withstand challenges and setbacks.

Recruitment and Retention of Skilled Individuals: Acknowledging the significance of attracting and maintaining highly skilled individuals. Promoting social responsibility and ethical practices as an employer improves the company's capacity to attract highly trained workers and cultivates employee loyalty.

Economic viability: Ensuring enduring financial stability and prosperity. Ensuring the company's ability to make beneficial contributions to society necessitates the careful management of both social and moral responsibilities alongside financial performance.

Reputation of a brand: Establishing and protecting a favourable brand image. An effective corporate citizenship strategy improves the value of a brand, leading to increased consumer loyalty and market competitiveness.

Good corporate citizenship entails the seamless incorporation of ethical principles, social accountability, and strategic business deliberations. Businesses that actively adopt and fulfil their social and moral responsibilities, while still prioritising long-term sustainability, are more likely to succeed in a dynamic and socially aware business environment.

II. Ethics and human rights

Within the framework of Corporate Social Responsibility (CSR), it is imperative to prioritise ethical considerations, safeguard human rights, and foster a harmonious global ecosystem as fundamental elements of responsible business practices. Companies that incorporate these elements into their corporate social responsibility (CSR) programmes make a significant contribution to fostering a more sustainable and equitable global business environment. Below is an analysis of each of these components:

1. Moral principles and values:

A. Clear and unambiguous business practices: Corporate Social Responsibility (CSR) entails upholding transparency in business operations, financial transactions, and communication with stakeholders. Adhering to ethical standards guarantees the precision of information and fosters confidence among stakeholders towards the organisation.

B. Ethical Employment Standards: Ensuring ethical treatment of employees encompasses providing equitable compensation, secure working environments, and avenues for career growth. Prioritising ethical labour practices boosts employee morale and fosters a positive organisational culture.

C. Measures to combat corruption: Companies dedicated to corporate social responsibility (CSR) proactively participate in efforts to combat corruption. Enforcing and advocating for anti-corruption laws guarantees equitable competition and protects the integrity of economic activities.

D. Involvement of relevant parties: Ethical corporate social responsibility (CSR) entails actively involving stakeholders, such as local communities, in order to comprehensively grasp their requirements and concerns. Transparent and sincere communication cultivates trust and nurtures constructive partnerships.

2. Rights of individuals:

A. Promoting a diverse and inclusive work environment: CSR programmes foster workplace diversity and inclusion, guaranteeing equitable opportunities for all employees. Ensuring and maintaining human rights in the workplace is essential for ethical corporate practices.

B. Responsibility in the Supply Chain: Companies demonstrate their dedication to human rights by guaranteeing responsible practices across the whole supply chain. This entails overseeing suppliers to ensure adherence to equitable labour practices and refraining from procuring from businesses involved in human rights transgressions.

C. Socioeconomic Progress: CSR programmes frequently incorporate efforts that actively contribute to the welfare of nearby communities. This entails providing assistance to education, healthcare, and social programmes that uplift marginalised groups and advocate for human rights.

D. Ethical Advertising Strategies: Companies dedicated to upholding human rights refrain from participating in discriminatory or exploitative marketing strategies. Incorporating ethical practices into advertising and avoiding the perpetuation of damaging stereotypes is an integral aspect of a competent corporate social responsibility (CSR) strategy.

III. Balance global environment

A. Environmental Sustainability: Corporate Social Responsibility (CSR) prioritises the implementation of ecologically sustainable practices. This include the reduction of carbon emissions, the minimization of waste, and the responsible utilisation of resources to alleviate the influence on the global environment.

B. Climate Action: Companies participate in corporate social responsibility (CSR) projects that are in line with worldwide endeavours to tackle climate change. This entails establishing goals for reducing emissions, allocating resources to develop renewable energy sources, and actively participating in international efforts to combat climate change.

C. Responsible Product Design: CSR encompasses product design, promoting the development of products that have a negligible environmental footprint over their entire lifespan. This encompasses the evaluation of the origins of raw materials, the methods used in production, and the proper handling and disposal of products at the end of their useful life.

D. Global Partnerships for Sustainability: Engaging in collaboration with international partners to tackle environmental concerns is a fundamental component of corporate social responsibility (CSR). This may entail engaging in international efforts, exchanging exemplary methods, and making contributions to the worldwide discourse on sustainable development.

Advantages of including ethics, human rights, and a balanced global environment in corporate social responsibility (CSR):

Improved Reputation: Organizations that place a high importance on ethics, human rights, and environmental stewardship cultivate a favourable reputation, which in turn draws socially aware consumers and investors.

Risk Mitigation: Proactively addressing ethical and human rights concerns helps to minimise potential damage to reputation and legal liabilities, thereby promoting the long-term survival of the business.

Global Competitiveness: Companies that adhere to international norms of ethics, human rights, and environmental sustainability have a strategic advantage in the global market, as they are able to attract a wide and varied consumer demographic.

Employee Satisfaction and Retention: Promoting a strong workplace culture that upholds ethics, human rights, and environmental responsibility is crucial for fostering employee satisfaction and ensuring staff retention.

Legal Compliance: CSR activities that specifically target ethical and human rights concerns guarantee adherence to both domestic and global legislation, thereby mitigating the likelihood of legal repercussions.

Social Licence to Operate: Companies that actively contribute to a harmonious global environment and uphold moral principles acquire the social licence to operate, cultivating favourable relationships with communities and stakeholders.

Ultimately, the incorporation of ethical principles, human rights considerations, and a dedication to maintaining a harmonious global environment in corporate social responsibility (CSR) efforts fosters a responsible and enduring business ecosystem. This approach not only conforms to cultural standards but also positions corporations as ethical frontrunners in a global economy that highly regards social and environmental accountability.

Environmentally responsible CSR

Within the framework of Corporate Social Responsibility (CSR), it is essential to prioritise the mitigation of global warming and the promotion of responsible utilisation of natural resources as integral elements of sustainable business strategies. Corporate social responsibility (CSR) activities that prioritise environmental stewardship play a crucial role in reducing the impact of climate change and advocating for responsible management of resources. Below is an analysis of how Corporate Social **Responsibility (CSR) might effectively tackle these concerns:**

Global warming concerns (Carbon footprint reduction): Corporate social responsibility (CSR) entails firms implementing measures to decrease their carbon footprint. This include the implementation of energy-efficient methodologies, allocation of resources towards renewable energy sources, and establishment of ambitious goals for reducing emissions.

Adaptation Strategies: Companies have the ability to incorporate adaptation strategies into their Corporate Social Responsibility (CSR) projects, particularly if their operations are located in places that are susceptible to the consequences of global warming. This may entail the construction of robust infrastructure or the provision of assistance to community projects aimed at adapting to climate change.

Climate Education and Advocacy: CSR initiatives can prioritise the dissemination of knowledge to employees, customers, and the wider society regarding the ramifications of global warming. Promoting climate action at the local, national, and global levels is a crucial component of corporate social responsibility (CSR) in response to climate change.

Green Supply Chain Practices: Companies can strive to mitigate the ecological footprint of their supply chains. This entails engaging in cooperative efforts with suppliers to implement sustainable practices, mitigate transportation emissions, and minimise waste generation.

Optimal Utilisation of Natural Resources: Sustainable sourcing is promoted by CSR as a means for organisations to implement environmentally responsible procurement practices. This entails the conscientious administration of the extraction of natural resources, guaranteeing the preservation of biodiversity, and reducing the environmental consequences of resource extraction.

Circular Economy Practices: Companies have the option to adopt circular economy principles, which entail including recyclability into product design, encouraging reuse, and minimising waste. The objective of this technique is to maximise the lifespan of materials.

Water management: Water conservation is promoted through CSR programmes, which involve developing strategies to use water resources wisely in operations and across the supply chain. Companies can also participate in community initiatives that advocate for appropriate water management.

Deforestation Reduction: Companies dedicated to corporate social responsibility (CSR) actively strive to diminish deforestation by procuring items like timber and palm oil from sustainable and certified origins. This endeavour facilitates the protection of biodiversity and the maintenance of ecosystems.

Incorporation into Corporate Social Responsibility (CSR) Initiatives:

Establishing Environmental Objectives: Corporate Social Responsibility (CSR) entails establishing precise environmental objectives that focus on lowering greenhouse gas emissions, minimising waste generation, and optimising resource utilisation. These objectives must be quantifiable and in accordance with global benchmarks.

Transparency and accountability: Companies dedicated to corporate social responsibility (CSR) frequently provide reports on their environmental performance to ensure transparency and accountability. Transparent reporting fosters accountability towards stakeholders and offers valuable insights into the advancement of environmental efforts.

Engaging Stakeholders: Corporate Social Responsibility (CSR) involves actively involving different stakeholders, including employees, consumers, and local communities, to ensure that environmental issues are taken into account when making decisions. This fosters a collaborative endeavour aimed at achieving sustainability.

Investment in innovation: Allocating funds from corporate social responsibility budgets to research and development enables companies to invest in the creation of groundbreaking solutions that promote environmental sustainability. This may entail the creation of environmentally sustainable products, procedures, or technologies.

Advantages of Corporate Social Responsibility (CSR) in Mitigating Global Warming and Managing Resource Utilisation:

Improved Brand Reputation: Companies that proactively tackle issues related to global warming and resource consumption through corporate social responsibility (CSR) activities cultivate a favourable brand reputation, attracting environmentally aware consumers.

Risk Mitigation: Corporate Social Responsibility (CSR) aids in reducing the likelihood and impact of risks related to environmental concerns, including potential fines imposed by regulations, harm to reputation, and disruptions in the supply chain caused by limited resources.

Cost Savings: Implementing sustainable practices frequently results in long-term cost reductions. Financial sustainability is achieved through energy-efficient operations, waste minimization, and prudent resource management.

Attracting and Retaining Talent: Demonstrating a dedication to Corporate Social Responsibility (CSR), particularly in solving environmental issues, appeals to employees who prioritise sustainability.

This enhances the ability to retain talented individuals and fosters a healthy business culture.

Community and Stakeholder Relations: Companies that proactively address environmental problems in their Corporate societal Responsibility (CSR) activities cultivate deeper relationships with local communities and stakeholders, thereby promoting a beneficial societal influence.

Ultimately, corporate social responsibility (CSR) endeavours that tackle the issue of global warming and advocate for the prudent use of natural resources play a significant role in establishing a company model that is both sustainable and accountable. By integrating corporate operations with environmental stewardship, firms not only satisfy their ethical obligations but also position themselves for enduring success in a world where environmental sustainability is progressively esteemed.

Chapter 7

Corporate Ethics

Corporate ethics include the moral principles and ideals that govern the conduct of a company organisation and its workers. Corporate responsibility is engaging in ethical and conscientious business practices, taking into account the consequences of actions on several stakeholders, including as employees, customers, suppliers, shareholders, and the wider community.

Crucial elements of corporate ethics encompass:

Integrity: integrity refers to the commitment to maintaining honesty and transparency in every business transaction. This entails refraining from engaging in deceptive activities and ensuring that the information conveyed to stakeholders is precise and honest.

Fairness: It refers to the practice of treating all stakeholders in a just and impartial manner. This applies to employees, customers, suppliers, and competitors as well. Implementing equitable policies and procedures enhances the reputation of a company and fosters confidence among all parties involved.

Stakeholder Respect: Recognising and honouring the interests and rights of all stakeholders. This encompasses the principles of valuing and upholding diversity, safeguarding human rights, and fostering a secure and all-encompassing work environment.

Compliance with law and regulations: Ensuring conformity with both domestic and global laws and regulations that regulate corporate activities. This guarantees that the company functions within the confines of the law and refrains from participating in unethical or unlawful practices.

Social responsibility: It refers to the acknowledgement and mitigation of the influence that corporate operations have on the wider society and the natural surroundings. This include endeavours such as corporate social responsibility (CSR) projects, sustainable practices, and philanthropic activities.

Accountability: it refers to the practice of ensuring that both individuals and the organisation are held responsible for their actions. This entails the establishment of procedures to denounce unethical conduct and the implementation of repercussions for breaches of ethical norms.

Corporate Governance: Establishing efficient governance frameworks to ensure accountable decision-making and supervision. This entails implementing a clearly defined system of checks and balances, with distinct roles and responsibilities assigned to executives and the board of directors.

Whistleblower Protection: Promoting a culture that fosters employees' confidence in disclosing unethical conduct without apprehension of reprisal. Safeguarding whistleblowers facilitates the exposure and resolution of ethical concerns within the organisation.

Ethical Leadership: Exemplifying ethical conduct throughout the entire organisation, commencing with uppermost leadership. Ethical leaders provide the prevailing atmosphere for the entire organisational culture, exerting influence on employees to behave with honesty and accountability.

By abiding by these principles, organisations can actively contribute to the establishment of trust, cultivating favourable relationships with stakeholders, and establishing a sustainable and accountable corporate environment. Adopting business ethics not only enhances the company's reputation but also fosters long-term prosperity and the welfare of the wider community.

Fundamental principles of ethics

The fundamental principles of ethics offer a structure for individuals and organisations to make morally upright choices and behave in an ethical fashion. Below are few essential foundational principles:

Autonomy: Respecting the autonomy of persons entails recognising their entitlement to exercise independent judgement and make self-determined judgements. This principle underscores the significance of obtaining consent based on adequate information and refraining from any type of coercion.

Nonmaleficence: This principle centres on the duty to avoid causing damage. It is important for individuals and organisations to make efforts to minimise harm and proactively avert any adverse outcomes that may arise from their actions.

Beneficence: This concept stresses actively promoting well-being and doing good deeds, going beyond the nonmaleficence principle. It promotes behaviours that actively contribute to the well-being of others.

Justice: The concept of justice entails the fair and equitable treatment of individuals. It prioritises the equitable allocation of advantages and disadvantages without any form of discrimination.

Fidelity: often known as faithfulness, emphasises the need of upholding commitments and being reliable. It entails upholding loyalty, honesty, and integrity in relationships and commitments.

Veracity: Veracity refers to the fundamental notion of being truthful. The text underscores the significance of practicing honesty and transparency in communication, while avoiding deceit or misleading information.

Confidentiality: Confidentiality entails the protection of private and sensitive information disclosed by persons. This principle is especially vital in professions such as healthcare, law, and counselling.

Accountability: Accountability refers to the fundamental concept of assuming responsibility for one's actions and decisions. It is important for individuals and organisations to be prepared to provide a rationale for their actions and be receptive to examination.

Integrity: Integrity refers to the act of consistently and ethically making decisions based on a set of principles. It necessitates the synchronisation of actions with ethical principles and benchmarks.

Respect for others: The fundamental principle of respecting others is acknowledging the intrinsic value and dignity of each person. This idea promotes the practice of treating others with politeness, compassion, and comprehension.

These core concepts establish a strong basis for ethical thinking and conduct. They provide guidance to individuals and organisations in dealing with intricate ethical challenges, promoting a culture characterised by honesty, confidence, and social accountability. By adhering to these values, decisions and actions are made with careful consideration for the welfare and rights of all parties concerned.

Concept of Values

Values can be defined as long-lasting ideas or principles that influence individuals' decisions and behaviours. They function as a fundamental basis for ethical decision-making, exerting an impact on behaviour and moulding individual and community standards.

Values have a consistent and enduring quality, remaining steadfast throughout an individual's lifetime. They offer a feeling of coherence and uniformity in one's convictions and behaviours.

Values are subjective and can differ among individuals, cultures, and societies. Individuals may have varying values, resulting in a range of viewpoints regarding what is considered significant.

Values exert a substantial influence on determining behaviour. They serve as intrinsic benchmarks that direct individuals in decision-making, establishing priorities, and assessing the importance of different facets of life.

Types of Values:

1. Personal Values: These encompass individual ideas and concepts that serve as a compass for personal conduct and decision-making. Personal values encompass virtues such as honesty, integrity, loyalty, and personal development.

2. Cultural Values: Collective convictions and standards that are commonly held within a specific culture. Societal expectations, conventions, and traditions are shaped by cultural values. Illustrative instances encompass reverence for the elderly or the significance of communal bonds.

3. Social Values: Social values are derived from interactions within social groupings and have a significant influence on collective behaviour. Examples of social values encompass principles such as fairness, parity, and collaboration.

B Moral values pertain to the principles of correct and incorrect conduct. Moral principles direct the process of making ethical choices and are frequently shaped by religious, philosophical, or cultural convictions.

5. Instrumental Values: These values pertain to the means or approaches considered significant in attaining objectives. Illustrative instances encompass diligent effort, accountability, and steadfastness.

6. Intrinsic Values: Values that are fundamentally desirable in and of themselves, regardless of any external rewards. Intrinsic values encompass happiness, love, and personal fulfilment.

Formation of Values:

1. Family and Upbringing: Early experiences within the family play a crucial role in shaping one's values. Parents and carers have a vital role in imparting moral and cultural values.

2. Social Environment: Engagements with peers, educational institutions, communities, and wider social frameworks shape one's values. Interactions with others influence one's viewpoints on working together, competing, and societal standards.

3. Cultural Influences: Cultural heritage and customs have a significant impact on the formation of values. Cultural institutions, religious rituals, and historical events foster the formation of collective values within a community.

4. Personal Experiences: Life events, difficulties, and achievements have the potential to influence an individual's values. Adversity can foster the cultivation of resilience as a fundamental principle, for instance.

5. Media and Technology: Mass media, encompassing television, internet, and social media, play a role in influencing values by presenting and reinforcing specific norms and behaviours.

6. Educational Institutions: Formal education exposes individuals to a variety of viewpoints, moral deliberations, and analytical reasoning. Educational institutions have a significant influence on the development of values pertaining to knowledge, intellectual inquisitiveness, and social accountability.

Gaining knowledge of values, their classifications, and the process of their development offers valuable understanding of the influences that contribute to the formation of personal and group ideas. Values function as fundamental beliefs that shape decision-making and behaviour across different domains of life.

Principles and concepts of managerial ethics

Managerial ethics pertains to the application of ethical ideas and concepts in the context of management and decision-making inside organisations. Below is a concise summary of the fundamental principles and concepts:

Foundations of Managerial Ethics:

1. Integrity: Managers should exhibit ethical behaviour and communicate openly and honestly. Upholding integrity entails practicing veracity, demonstrating unwavering constancy in behaviour, and adhering to moral and ethical principles.

2. Responsibility: Managers are obligated to assess the consequences of their decisions on different stakeholders, such as employees, customers, shareholders, and the community. This principle highlights the importance of holding managers responsible for the outcomes of their activities.

3. Equity: Ensuring impartial treatment of all employees and stakeholders is of utmost importance. This concept promotes equality and opposes any sort of bias, favouritism, or unjust treatment inside the organisation.

4. Transparency: Transparent communication guarantees the disclosure of pertinent information to stakeholders. Transparency fosters confidence and facilitates the maintenance of candid and open interactions inside the organisation.

5. Individual Respect: Managers must demonstrate reverence for the dignity, entitlements, and variety of persons within the organisation. Establishing a culture characterised by respect cultivates a work atmosphere that is both positive and inclusive.

6. Loyalty: Managers must exhibit allegiance to the organisation and its objectives. This entails giving precedence to the interests of the organisation and its stakeholders over personal interests.

7. Integrity: Exhibiting honesty and directness in communication is essential. Transparent communication cultivates confidence among employees and stakeholders.

8. Corporate Citizenship: Managers should examine the influence of their decisions on the broader community and environment. This entails actively participating in socially responsible initiatives and making meaningful contributions to the betterment of society.

Principles of Ethical Management:

1. Ethical Decision-Making: The systematic assessment and selection of activities that are in accordance with ethical ideals. Managers ought to contemplate the possible ramifications and moral implications of their decisions.

2. Code of Conduct: A comprehensive set of principles or regulations that delineates the anticipated conduct inside the organisation. An explicitly specified code of conduct serves to establish ethical benchmarks for both employees and management.

3. Whistle blowing: Promoting a culture where employees are empowered to expose unethical conduct without facing any form of reprisal. Whistleblowing systems facilitate the exposure and resolution of ethical infractions within the organisation.

4. Corporate Social Responsibility (CSR): The notion that firms bear an obligation to make constructive contributions to society. Corporate Social Responsibility (CSR) include the implementation of ethical principles, philanthropic activities, and ecologically friendly initiatives.

5. Stakeholder Management: Acknowledging the interests and concerns of different stakeholders and effectively balancing them during the decision-making process. Stakeholder management ensures that decisions take into account the welfare of all pertinent parties.

6. Ethical Leadership: Managers must serve as role models, exhibiting ethical conduct and cultivating a climate of honesty and moral principles throughout the organisation. Effective leadership has a significant impact on the ethical atmosphere within the workplace.

7. Corporate Governance: Creating frameworks and procedures to ensure efficient decision-making, responsibility, and supervision inside the company. Effective corporate governance serves as a deterrent against unethical conduct and guarantees responsible leadership.

Managers may foster a culture of integrity, trust, and ethical behaviour inside their organisations by integrating these principles and concepts into their decision-making processes.

Ethics and values in business

The significance of ethics and values in business is of utmost importance, since they have a profound impact on organisational culture, decision-making processes, and long-term performance. Below is an in-depth analysis of their importance:

1. Organisational Culture: Culture within an organisation is formed by the influence of ethics and values. Embracing ethical standards among leaders and employees cultivates a favourable and all-encompassing work atmosphere.

Employee involvement: A robust ethical culture enhances employee morale and fosters greater involvement. Employees experience a strong feeling of purpose and a harmonious connection with the organization's ideals.

2. Decision-Making Processes:

Principles to Guide Decision-Making: Ethics offer a framework of fundamental principles to guide decision-making. When confronted with moral issues, adhering to ethical values guarantees that decisions are in accordance with moral principles.

Long-term perspective: Ethical decision-making takes into account the enduring consequences for the organisation, stakeholders, and society. It contributes to the establishment of trust and long-term viability.

3. Customer Trust and Loyalty:

Brand Reputation: Enterprises renowned for their ethical activities cultivate a favourable brand reputation. Customers are more inclined to place faith in and maintain loyalty towards organisations that prioritise ethics and values.

Consumer Choices: Ethical issues are playing a growing role in shaping consumer decisions. Companies that place a high importance on social responsibility and ethical conduct tend to appeal to a wider range of customers.

4. Employee Recruitment and Retention:

Talent Acquisition: Companies that possess a robust ethical framework are able to attract highly skilled individuals. Prospective employees are looking for workplaces that are in accordance with their personal ideals.

Employee retention rates are generally higher in ethical organisations. Organisations that prioritise the well-being and ethical conduct of their employees are more likely to retain them.

5. Stakeholder Relationships:

Establishing Trust with Stakeholders: Engaging in ethical conduct fosters trust among diverse stakeholders, including as investors, suppliers, and the community. Trust is essential for establishing and maintaining long-term partnerships and collaborations.

Minimising Risks: Adhering to ethical business practices decreases the likelihood of encountering legal complications, regulatory obstacles, and harm to relationships with stakeholders.

6. Ensuring adherence to laws and regulations:

Minimizing potential risks: Conforming to ethical standards frequently coincides with legal and regulatory obligations. Engaging in ethical conduct reduces legal liabilities and guarantees adherence to industry norms.

Preventing Scandals: Engaging in unethical conduct can result in legal complications and scandals, which can harm the business's brand. Engaging in ethical behaviour serves as a proactive approach to avoid legal complications.

7. Corporate Social Responsibility (CSR):

Impact on the Community: Incorporating ethical principles encompasses the concept of corporate social responsibility. Businesses make beneficial contributions to the community through philanthropic endeavours, environmental sustainability efforts, and social projects.

Sustainable Practices: Ethical business practices play a role in promoting sustainable development by addressing both environmental and social problems.

8. Risk Management:

Reputation Risk: Upholding ethical standards reduces reputation risk. The negative impact of a damaged reputation on a corporation can be significant, leading to decreased consumer trust, diminished investor confidence, and reduced market competitiveness.

Financial Risks: Ethical breaches can result in financial liabilities, such as litigation, penalties, and missed commercial prospects. Ethical risk management serves as a protective measure against these possible drawbacks.

Essentially, ethics and values serve as fundamental pillars for the prosperity and longevity of businesses. They establish a favourable organisational culture, direct decision-making, cultivate stakeholder confidence, and lead to sustained profitability. Companies that give priority to ethical behaviour not only handle difficulties more efficiently but also have a crucial impact on constructing a conscientious and enduring worldwide economy.

Corruption in business

Corruption in the business sector pertains to the exploitation of authority or position for personal benefit, usually comprising deceitful or unethical conduct within an organisational framework. It can manifest in diverse ways and has extensive ramifications for individuals, corporations, and society. Below is an analysis of corruption within the corporate sector:

1. Types of Corporate Corruption:

A.   Bribery refers to the act of providing, presenting, accepting, or requesting something valuable with the intention of exerting influence on the decisions or behaviour of a person in a position of power or authority.

B.   Embezzlement refers to the act of unlawfully diverting monies that have been entrusted to an individual, typically an employee, for their personal gain.

C.   Fraud refers to the use of deceptive tactics with the aim of obtaining unfair or illegal benefits, such as misrepresenting financial information or manipulating it.

D.   Kickbacks refer to clandestine payments given to individuals in exchange for preferential treatment, contracts, or business agreements.

2. Factors contributing to corruption in the business sector:

Insufficient Ethical Leadership: When executives in an organisation participate in or permit unethical conduct, it can establish a precedent for corruption among employees.

Insufficient regulatory frameworks: Insatisfactory legislation and enforcement mechanisms create conditions that facilitate the proliferation of corrupt behaviours.

Organisations that do not have openness in their financial transactions and decision-making are more prone to corruption.

Cultural and societal factors: Cultural norms that exhibit tolerance or even endorsement of corruption can foster an atmosphere where unethical practices are more prone to transpire.

3. Implications of Corporate Corruption:

Reputation Impairment: Enterprises engaged in corrupt practices experience substantial impairment to their reputation, resulting in diminished trust from customers, partners, and the general public.

Legal Ramifications: Engaging in corrupt practices can lead to legal proceedings, monetary sanctions, and penalties, which can adversely affect the financial solvency of the business.

Economic Impact: Corruption impedes economic progress by distorting market mechanisms, discouraging investment, and promoting inequality.

Adverse Organisational Culture: The prevalence of corruption can become deeply rooted in the organisational culture, sustaining unethical conduct.

4. Strategies to Counteract Business Corruption:

Enforcing Ethical principles: Companies should adopt and enforce unambiguous ethical principles, prioritising honesty, openness, and responsibility.

Whistleblower Protection: Promoting and safeguarding individuals who expose corrupt practices within the organisation aids in the discovery and resolution of concerns.

Stringent legal frameworks: Enhancing legal frameworks and maintaining stringent enforcement of anti-corruption laws is crucial to discourage illicit practices.

Advocating for Transparency: The practice of being transparent in financial transactions, decision-making processes, and corporate governance serves as a deterrent against corruption.

5. Global Efforts to Combat Corruption:

The United Nations Convention Against Corruption (UNCAC) is an international convention aimed at combating corruption on a global scale, offering a comprehensive framework for addressing this issue.

Transparency International is a worldwide non-governmental organisation that specifically targets corruption by doing research, engaging in advocacy, and implementing anti-corruption measures.

6. The role of Corporate Social Responsibility (CSR) in addressing corruption:

Promoting ethical conduct in business: Integrating ethical issues into corporate operations and supply chains is an essential component of Corporate Social Responsibility (CSR).

Businesses have the ability to actively engage in and endorse efforts that try to tackle corruption on a larger scope.

To tackle corruption in organisations, a comprehensive strategy is needed that encompasses ethical leadership, legal frameworks, and societal transformation. Embracing openness, accountability, and ethical behaviour is crucial for cultivating a business atmosphere devoid of corrupt practices.

Chapter 8

Ethics and Indian managers

Indian managers' values are influenced by a blend of cultural, societal, and personal factors. India, renowned for its abundant cultural past and varied traditions, showcases a distinctive array of values that frequently impact managerial methodologies. Below are few prevalent values frequently noticed among Indian managers:

1. Hierarchy and Authority: Indian culture highly values hierarchy and authority. Managers frequently have a profound reverence for hierarchical frameworks inside organisations, which is evident in their leadership approach.

2. Family and Community Values: The Indian culture places great importance on the function of family. Indian managers frequently prioritise family values and carry this communal spirit to the workplace, producing a supportive and familial environment.

3. Cultural Sensitivity: India's multifaceted cultural milieu underscores the significance of comprehending and valuing cultural disparities. Indian managers frequently demonstrate a notable level of cultural sensitivity, placing a strong emphasis on valuing diversity within the workplace.

4. Long-Term partnerships: Indian managers commonly prioritise the establishment and sustenance of enduring partnerships. Business connections are commonly perceived as collaborative partnerships that go beyond immediate transactions.

5. Collectivism: Indian society typically exhibits a collectivist orientation, prioritising the unity and cooperation of groups. Indian managers frequently prioritise the success of the team over individual accomplishments, cultivating a sense of cohesion and common objectives.

6. Spirituality and Ethics: Numerous Indian managers include spiritual and ethical beliefs into their decision-making process. Principles like as dharma (moral duty) and karma (cause and effect) can impact their ethical deliberations.

7. Work-Life Balance: Although Indian managers uphold a strong work ethic, they frequently acknowledge the significance of maintaining a healthy work-life balance. This exemplifies the cultural focus on comprehensive well-being, encompassing physical, mental, and emotional dimensions.

8. Adaptability: The ability of managers to adapt is highly valued in India, as it reflects the country's history of being able to adjust and bounce back from challenges. Adaptability is frequently regarded as a crucial asset when it comes to addressing evolving situations.

9. Inclusiveness: Indian managers frequently demonstrate a commitment to inclusivity. This is seen in endeavours to incorporate a wide range of viewpoints, genders, and backgrounds in the processes of making decisions.

10. Humility: Humility is highly esteemed in Indian culture, and numerous managers demonstrate modesty and humility in their dealings. This is evident in their leadership style, as they frequently prioritise collective accomplishments over individual recognition.

11. Dedication to Education: Education holds great importance in Indian culture, which is evident in the strong focus on ongoing learning and growth among Indian managers.

12. Indian managers: exhibit a pervasive and robust sense of patriotism and nationalism. This could impact corporate decisions that are in line with the interests of the nation.

It is crucial to acknowledge that although these values offer broad perspectives, there is considerable heterogeneity among Indian managers, and individual values may differ depending on factors such as geographical location, industry, and personal upbringing. Furthermore, the values of Indian managers are being influenced by globalisation and exposure to international corporate practices, resulting in a dynamic and ever-changing management landscape.

Factors influencing business ethics

Business ethics are influenced by a variety of issues, which demonstrate the intricate interaction between internal and external forces on organisations. The following are crucial determinants that impact business ethics:

1. Internal Factors:

A. Leadership: The ethical ideals and conduct of senior leadership have a substantial influence on the ethical culture within an organisation. Leaders establish the prevailing ethical norms and guide the process of making decisions.

B. Organisational Culture: The dominant culture within an organisation influences the ethical conduct of its members. An organisational culture that promotes transparency, honesty, and integrity cultivates ethical behaviour among personnel.

C. Structure of an organisation: The organisational structure, encompassing its hierarchical relationships and mechanisms for decision-making, might impact the probability of ethical conduct. An explicit and transparent framework facilitates the practice of moral behaviour.

D. Ethical policies and codes: Formal ethical principles and codes of conduct offer employees clear instructions. The presence and implementation of such policies have an impact on the ethical decision-making process within the organisation.

E. Education and enhancement: Employee training programmes that provide emphasis on ethical issues foster an organisational culture that esteems and places high importance on ethical conduct.

F. Systems for evaluating and assessing employee performance: The selection criteria employed in performance evaluations can have a significant influence on ethical conduct. Emphasising both financial and ethical performance effectively communicates the organization's priorities.

2. External Factors:

A. Legal and regulatory framework: The legislative framework and regulatory environment establish a baseline for ethical conduct that businesses must adhere to. Adherence to laws and regulations is a crucial component of ethical behaviour.

B. Economic circumstances: Economic variables, such as market rivalry and fiscal constraints, have the potential to impact ethical decision-making. Organisations encountering financial difficulties may confront ethical quandaries while striving for profitability.

C. Stakeholder expectations: Ethical considerations are influenced by the expectations of different stakeholders, such as consumers, employees, investors, and the community. Organisations frequently synchronise their actions with the expectations of stakeholders in order to uphold confidence.

D. Globalisation: Globalisation refers to the process of increasing interconnectedness and interdependence among countries, economies, and societies worldwide.

Conducting business in a globalised setting exposes companies to a wide range of cultural and ethical standards. International businesses must prioritise adapting to diverse ethical requirements in different regions.

E. The relationship between media and public opinion: The reputation of an organisation can be greatly influenced by public scrutiny and media attention. Unethical actions can result in negative press, which can significantly impact brand image and erode customer trust.

F. Social and cultural influences: Ethical standards are influenced by societal and cultural norms. Organisations that operate in different cultures must take into account and show respect for the cultural subtleties that influence ethical standards.

G. Technological Progress: Technology presents novel ethical dilemmas, including concerns around data privacy, cybersecurity, and the conscientious utilisation of evolving technologies. As technology advances, ethical considerations must also progress.

H. Intense market forces: Organisations may feel compelled to sacrifice ethical norms in order to achieve a competitive edge due to the influence of the competitive landscape. Ensuring ethical practices in a competitive market necessitates deliberate exertion.

I. Ecological Issues: The growing recognition of environmental concerns has resulted in a concentration on sustainable and ethical business strategies. Organisations are required to assess their ecological footprint and embrace ethical environmental practices.

J. Supplier and Business Partner Relationships: An organization's reputation can be influenced by the ethical behaviour of its suppliers and business partners. Engaging in ethical sourcing and collaborating with ethical partners are key factors that enhance the overall integrity of an organisation.

Comprehending and manoeuvring through these internal and external forces is vital for organisations to build and uphold a robust ethical framework, promoting a culture of honesty and accountable business behaviour.

Role of international trade and business organizations in CSR

The significance of international trade and corporate organisations in Corporate Social Responsibility (CSR) has grown as global commerce continues to increase. CSR, or Corporate Social Responsibility, denotes a company's dedication to tackling social, environmental, and ethical issues alongside the pursuit of economic objectives. International trade and business organisations contribute to Corporate Social Responsibility (CSR) in the following ways:

1. Global Standards and Guidelines: International trade organisations, such as the World Trade Organisation (WTO), frequently cooperate with business associations to create worldwide corporate social responsibility (CSR) standards and guidelines. These frameworks serve as a basis for ethical and responsible business activities.

2. Advocacy and Awareness: Business organisations, such as chambers of commerce and trade groups, have a responsibility to promote and support the implementation of CSR principles. Their objective is to promote consciousness of the significance of ethical behaviour and to urge member companies to adopt responsible business practices.

3. Collaboration and Partnerships: International business organisations promote the cooperation and alliances between firms, non-governmental organisations (NGOs), governments, and other relevant parties. These partnerships amplify the influence of corporate social responsibility programmes by combining resources and expertise.

4. Capacity Building: Business organisations facilitate capacity building activities to assist enterprises in incorporating CSR into their operations. This encompasses offering instruction, materials, and direction on executing enduring and ethically accountable measures.

5. CSR Reporting Standards: Organizations such as the Global Reporting Initiative (GRI) are responsible for creating and advocating for standards that govern the reporting of corporate social responsibility (CSR) activities. These standards provide guidance to firms on how to disclose their social, environmental, and economic performance, promoting transparency and responsibility.

6. Implementing Sustainable Practices: Trade organisations promote the adoption of environmentally-friendly corporate practices. This entails advocating for ecologically sustainable initiatives, conscientious management of the supply chain, and ethical methods in sourcing.

7. Trade Agreements with CSR Components: Trade agreements often include corporate social responsibility (CSR) components. These agreements can incentivize member nations to comply with specific social and environmental criteria, thereby promoting ethical business conduct.

8. Global Compact Initiatives: The United Nations Global Compact encourages businesses around the world to implement sustainable and socially responsible strategies. Companies who engage in the Global Compact pledge to adhere to ten principles that encompass human rights, labour practices, environmental sustainability, and anti-corruption measures.

9. Ethical trading Initiatives: The Ethical Trading Initiative (ETI) and similar organisations aim to advance ethical trading practices. They collaborate with enterprises to guarantee equitable treatment of employees, ethical acquisition of resources, and compliance with labour regulations.

10. Supply chain sustainability: International trade organisations focus on supply chain sustainability, which involves promoting responsible procurement, fair labour practices, and environmental stewardship at every stage of the supply chain.

11. CSR Certifications and Labels: Different certifications and labels, supported by global organisations, indicate compliance with certain CSR standards. For instance, Fair Trade accreditation guarantees equitable remuneration and ethical manufacturing methods.

12. Promoting Community Development: Business organisations frequently endorse CSR programmes that actively contribute to the advancement of local communities. This may entail providing assistance to education, healthcare, and other social initiatives in the communities where corporations are established.

13. Responsible Investment Practices: International business organisations promote responsible investment practices, urging investors to incorporate environmental, social, and governance (ESG) factors into their decision-making.

International commerce and commercial organisations are essential in influencing the corporate social responsibility (CSR) environment. These organisations contribute to a more sustainable and ethical global business environment by implementing standards, encouraging collaboration, and advocating responsible corporate practices. Incorporating CSR concepts into international trade is crucial for effectively tackling social and environmental concerns at a global level.

Ombudsman

The Ombudsman, originating from Scandinavian customs, has developed into an institutional apparatus aimed at resolving complaints, conflicts, and matters pertaining to public administration, corporate conduct, and diverse organisations. Here is a concise summary of the concept:

1. Definition and Origin: The term "Ombudsman" has its roots in the Swedish language, where it signifies a "representative" or a "agent." The notion was initially introduced in Sweden in 1809 as a means to redress grievances raised by civilians against government officials. Currently, Ombudsman offices are present in diverse countries and industries.

2. Role and Function: An Ombudsman serves as an autonomous and unbiased intermediary between an individual and an organisation, typically a governmental entity or corporation. Their primary function is to examine grievances, promote the resolution of conflicts, and guarantee impartiality in decision-making procedures.

3. Independence and Impartiality: Ombudsmen are often autonomous bodies, distinct from the institutions they supervise. The autonomy of the evaluators guarantees impartiality and eliminates conflicts of interest, enabling them to assess complaints and concerns in an objective manner.

4. Confidentiality: Ombudsman offices frequently adhere to the idea of confidentiality. Complainants are able to express their grievances without any concern of facing retaliation, and the Ombudsman deals with matters in a confidential manner while actively pursuing solutions.

5. Accessibility: Ombudsmen are intended to be easily reachable by the general public. They offer a platform for those who perceive themselves as being harmed or treated unfairly to express their grievances without excessive bureaucracy or formal judicial procedures.

6. Jurisdictional Scope: Ombudsmen with authority over a broad array of matters, encompassing administrative rulings, infringements upon human rights, business conduct, and provision of public services. The extent of the Ombudsman office's authority depends on the precise mandate it has been given.

7. Ensuring Equity and Responsibility: Ombudsmen strive to guarantee that organisations and institutions function in a just and open manner. They ensure that decision-makers are held responsible for their actions and actively contribute to enhancing organisational processes and practices.

8. Educational Function: Ombudsmen frequently participate in educational endeavours aimed at fostering awareness regarding individuals' rights, ethical norms, and the operations of the Ombudsman office. This promotes proactive measures and fosters a culture of responsibility among organisations.

9. Variations in Ombudsman Models: Ombudsman models exhibit diversity in their structure and implementation, which might differ across different legal jurisdictions and sectors. Certain nations have established national Ombudsman offices to supervise public administration, but others may have specialised Ombudsmen dedicated to specialised sectors, such as healthcare or corporate affairs.

10. Non-Adversarial Approach: The Ombudsman process often avoids conflict and seeks to address issues by using mediation, negotiation, and facilitation methods instead than resorting to legal actions. This method encourages a collaborative resolution of conflicts.

11. Checks and Balances: Ombudsmen have a role in maintaining checks and balances in a system. By offering a platform for individuals to express complaints, they improve the responsibility, openness, and overall efficiency of organisations and institutions.

12. Continuous Improvement: Ombudsmen typically play a role in advocating systemic changes inside companies based on repeated issues. This aids to ongoing enhancement, promoting superior methodologies and averting future conflicts.

The notion of the Ombudsman has demonstrated its efficacy as a beneficial instrument in fostering equity, responsibility, and efficient conflict resolution in diverse contexts, hence enhancing the general well-being and operation of organisations and governmental institutions.

NGO and CSR

NGOs, also known as Non-Governmental Organisations, are private entities that function autonomously without government oversight. These organisations are usually non-profit and have a specific emphasis on tackling social, environmental, or humanitarian concerns.

Salient Features:

Non-Profit Orientation: NGOs are motivated by a purpose to tackle societal concerns rather than pursuing financial gains. Excess revenues are reinvested into the organization's mission.

Autonomy: Non-governmental organisations function autonomously, free from governmental interference, enabling them to champion social causes, tackle problems, and deliver services without being bound by political limitations.

Varied Areas of Emphasis: Non-governmental organisations encompass a broad spectrum of sectors, such as healthcare, education, environmental preservation, human rights, and other domains. Their areas of attention are contingent upon their mission and objectives.

Voluntary Membership: Membership in non-governmental organisations (NGOs) is generally based on voluntary participation, where individuals and organisations choose to join based on shared values and a dedication to the organization's objective.

Advocacy and Activism: Numerous non-governmental organisations (NGOs) actively participate in advocacy and activism endeavours with the aim of increasing public consciousness, exerting influence on policies, and fostering societal transformation. They frequently act as advocates for marginalised or underprivileged populations.

NGOs acquire funding from a range of sources, such as donations, grants, and collaborations. This varied funding model enables them to preserve their autonomy.

Summary of CSR (Corporate Social Responsibility)

Explanation: CSR, short for Corporate Social Responsibility, pertains to a company's dedication to achieving a harmonious equilibrium between economic objectives and social and environmental factors. It entails incorporating ethical and sustainable principles into the functioning of a firm.

Salient Features:

Voluntary Initiatives: CSR initiatives refer to deliberate and discretionary measures undertaken by businesses to make positive contributions to society. They surpass their legal obligations and consider the wider consequences of their commercial actions.

Triple Bottom Line: Corporate Social Responsibility (CSR) encompasses the principle of the "triple bottom line," which takes into account the social, environmental, and financial dimensions. Companies strive to generate value not alone for shareholders, but also for communities and the environment.

Sustainability Practices: Corporate Social Responsibility (CSR) frequently entails the implementation of sustainable practices, which encompass minimising the environmental footprint, advocating for ethical procurement, and guaranteeing equitable labour standards across the supply chain.

Community Engagement: Companies foster connections with communities through philanthropic initiatives, social initiatives, and collaborative partnerships. CSR initiatives strive to enhance the well-being of neighbouring communities and foster societal progress.

Stakeholder Consideration: Corporate Social Responsibility (CSR) prioritises the careful consideration of the concerns and interests of different stakeholders, such as consumers, employees, investors, and the wider community. Ensuring a careful equilibrium between these interests is crucial for practicing responsible business.

Transparency and Reporting: It is crucial to have clear and open communication on corporate social responsibility (CSR) efforts. Several corporations release Corporate Social Responsibility (CSR) reports that provide comprehensive information on their societal and environmental influence, objectives, and advancements.

Ethical leadership is strongly associated with Corporate Social Responsibility (CSR). Companies that possess robust ethical principles prioritise responsible behaviour, integrity, and responsibility in their commercial activities.

The relationship between NGOs and CSR involves a frequent collaboration between non-governmental organisations and enterprises in order to amplify the effectiveness of corporate social responsibility activities. Non-governmental organisations (NGOs) contribute specialised knowledge, local networks, and a profound comprehension of societal matters, while companies offer financial and logistical support and a platform to tackle these concerns.

Collaborations between non-governmental organisations (NGOs) and businesses have the potential to create more efficient and enduring corporate social responsibility (CSR) initiatives that tackle societal issues while also being in line with the values and objectives of the company.